Recreation From Behind Prison Walls

MICHAEL A. NORCROSS

To: Danny and Sherry

Best Wishes,

Mike

Copyright © 2014 Michael A. Norcross

All rights reserved.

ISBN:9781494357610

CHAPTERS

1. A History of Oklahoma State Reformatory
2. Recreation IS Rehabilitation
3. My Co-Workers-My Friends
4. Many Wardens, Deputy Wardens, Majors-Different Philosophies
5. The Old Gym-Our Playground
6. The Band-Musical Creativity
7. The Softball Field- Temporary Relief from Stress
8. All-Star Teams-What a Hassle!
9. Trips to Basketball and Softball Tournaments
10. The Rodeo-Money the Hard Way
11. A Sports Movie Similar to OSR Sports
12. We Can Take You Hostage Any Time
13. Any Inmate Can Get Killed
14. Any Employee Can Get Killed
15. An Escape or a Killing?
16. The Story of Killer
17. From Juvenile Delinquency and from Military to Criminal
18. "I'll Be Back"-High Recidivism Rate
19. Teachers Bring Their Students to Prison for an Education
20. Lawsuits Galore-Sued for Three Cans of Pop
21. Humor Is Good Medicine
22. Getting Punched in the Nose. "Ouch!" Boy, Did I Bleed
23. The Lifers Club-The Most Progressive Club
24. Cheating on Recreational Events
25. Games Played by Criminals
26. The Observance of the Verna Stafford Parole Hearing
27. The Lowest Status in a Prison
28. A 1973 Prison Riot
29. A 1980 Prison Riot
30. Bizarre Stories about Inmates, Probationers, and Parolees
31. Interesting Odds and Ends

MICHAEL A. NORCROSS

DEDICATION

I dedicate this book to Nelda, my wife, who helped me correct my mistakes on the computer as I was typing this book; Chris, my son, who encouraged me to write this book; Mika, my daughter, who formatted the manuscript of this book; my grandchildren, Kaylee, Blake, and Cooper who will someday this book will become a legacy to them, hopefully: and Randy and Joe Mitchell Norcross, my cousins, whose interest in Correctional Recreation kept my interest alive.

ACKNOWLEDGMENTS

Deatra Beavers, our niece, took the time to photograph the cover of this book.
Dakota Lewallen, our great-nephew, spent much time designing the cover of this book.
Cluster Rhodes, our uncle, gave me many ideas from a book that he had written.
Bobby Craft, my Supervisor at OSR and Dannie Blevins, my co-worker, shared experiences that inspired this book.
Nick Armstrong gave me stories about his experiences at OSR.
Paul Morris gave me much information from his own book.
Glenda Atkinson took much time editing this book in a professional manner.

INTRODUCTION

I, Michael Norcross, graduated from Southwestern Oklahoma State University in 1971 with a degree in Recreational Leadership/ Recreational Therapy. I worked eleven and a half years for the Oklahoma State Department of Human Services, six of those years coordinating recreation programs for juveniles. I worked twenty-three years as a Recreation Supervisor at the Oklahoma State Reformatory at Granite, Oklahoma, which is a prison under the Department of Corrections. I worked in a gym, usually by myself, with an average of one hundred fifty inmates a night. I retired from the Oklahoma Department of Corrections in December 2006. I spend much of my time attempting to oil paint classic cars and practicing the bass guitar hoping to play in a rock band. I live at Falconhead Resort in Oklahoma with Nelda, my wife of forty-two years.

The intent of this book is to offer a unique perspective of prison life from a recreation format. All of the stories are true, and the names are real names (except in chapter 25.) In thirty-one chapters, I try to portray many insights that a Recreation Supervisor encounters with inmates during recreational activities. I emphasize that prison can be one of the most dangerous places on earth; however, prison stories are very interesting to most people.

The ID badge that I wore to work for 23 years.

The plaque I received for 23 years of service at OSR. Actually, I received 24 years because I had a year of unused sick leave.

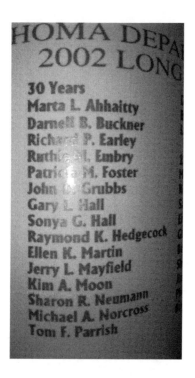

A cup that I got for 30 years of service at DHS and DOC in 2002.

I am practicing my bass guitar at my home at Falconhead Resort.

MICHAEL A. NORCROSS

Chapter 1
A HISTORY OF OKLAHOMA STATE REFORMATORY

Before I begin this book, I think that it is important to start with a history of OSR. This will lay a foundation prior to the implementation of recreation programs at OSR. The legislature in the Oklahoma Territory in 1890 authorized its Governor to have a contract with Kansas for the care of Oklahoma inmates at $38,000 per year. However, Kansas increased the cost per inmate to 50 cents per day. Oklahoma negotiated the bid to 35 cents and this remained intact until 1905, when the contractual fee was raised to 40 cents per inmate. Rising costs and rising populations of inmates caused some Oklahoma officials to question continuation of the contract with Kansas for the incarceration of inmates. An 1899 report to the Governor said that the inmate population had reached a high of 179. Four months into his administration Charles Haskell, the first Governor of the State of Oklahoma, recommended that the legislature appropriate funds to build a new penitentiary and reform school in the new state. He argued that convicts could work on the much needed repair on roads with free labor. By the end of the first session, the legislature authorized the Board of Prison Control to Purchase land at McAlester, Oklahoma, and to begin construction of a new penitentiary using convict labor. The first 100 inmates arrived from Lansing on October 14, 1908. They were housed at the McAlester jail. The inmates eventually built a stockade to house themselves. The building included a dining room, kitchen, and laundry. Governor Haskell reminded the legislature in January 1909 that the contract with Kansas would expire at the end of the month. He wanted to know the fate of 155 inmates at McAlester, over 562 at Lansing, and 150 in county jails.

The catalyst that changed the arrangement of sending convicted felons to Kansas was Kate Barnard, Oklahoma's first Commissioner of Charities and Corrections. She felt that a good prison was one that produced the largest percentage of prisoners who never returned to a life of crime. Her solution was to give the inmate medical and psychological treatment. She received numerous complaints about the treatment of inmates and the general conditions of the Kansas Penitentiary. Soon after her official duties began, she visited the prison at Lansing in August 1908. She arrived unannounced and joined sightseers, paid the normal admittance of 50 cents, and was shown the "showplaces" of the institution. She made a public report in December 1908 and demanded a full investigation. She charged the Kansas authorities with brutality, graft, and corruption in their operation of the prison. She said the prisoners were fed only one meal per day. Kate learned that from 1905 to 1908, 60 boys had been sent to Lansing who were under 16 years of age. She then recommended to the Governor and the legislators that all inmates at Lansing be immediately transferred from Lansing to Oklahoma. The legislature finally appropriated $850,000 to construct the penitentiary. After her retirement in

1946, the Department never developed a reputation for human reform as effective of Kate Barnard. She felt the state needed a reformatory for boys.

The first Warden of the reformatory was Samuel Flourney. He wrote a letter to the Governor and complained of discrimination in Southwestern Oklahoma for not having a reformatory. He requested a $100,000 appropriation. The Oklahoma State Reformatory was established by an act of the legislature in March 1909, with an appropriation of $500,000. The temporary quarters were built south of the "Wildcat" mountain. (Wildcat Mountain was the mountain that the inmates "busted rocks from" and subsequently sold the rocks to various companies. The guard tower still remains after all these years! It is on the National Register of Historic Places and will probably never be torn down. I tried to get a photograph of the old guard tower, but it was too far away.) The first 60 inmates were received from McAlester on April 22, 1910, and then 50 more in May. Two hundred more prisoners were transferred from McAlester on March 1911, and they all began public road work. Construction of the main facility began in 1911 and was completed in 1914. The temporary quarters were destroyed by fire the same year. During Kate Barnard's tenure, she founded, built, and implemented operations both in the penitentiary and the reformatory. She had lofty and realistic goals for both institutions and gave personal attention to the inmates. Governor Robert Williams (1915-1919), in his message to the legislature in 1917, was concerned about the economic status of the facility, in addition to rehabilitation. He made no distinction between the reformatory and the penitentiary. He said the reformatory at Granite was a penitentiary just as much as the prison at McAlester. He wanted to use the reformatory as a 2nd penitentiary. He wanted to use the state-owned "Wildcat" mountain of granite, as previously mentioned, and negotiated a contract with Rock Island Railroad Company. The railroad exchanged a small rock crusher (capable of 80 yards a day) for 1200 carloads of rough rock for its track beds. The Governor then said, "The reformatory is now self-sustaining." Within three years there was improvement of the prison gin machine, dairy barn, and power house machinery. There also was the building of a 20,000 bushel granary, the east cell house which was two-thirds completed, and a broom factory. (All of the actual cells and the mechanism which opened the cells were shipped from Cincinnati, Ohio.)

To assist the government in World War I, the prison supplied building materials to the Aviation Field at Fort Sill, Oklahoma. It was reported that 75 to 80 percent of the inmates released from there never returned to criminal life. The east cell house was completed in 1918 with four levels. The fourth level was an open area since construction had been utilized for many purposes, ranging from classrooms to open dormitory. It is now used as an exercise room for employees. This added 290 beds to the capacity of the prison. By the end of the year, the bed count of the institution was 658. During the next few years the reformatory got closer to its reformative ideal.

Governor James Robertson (1919-1923) made an honest effort to run the prison as a reformatory. He appointed as Warden, Dr. George A. Waters, who was a farmer and a dentist. Governor Robertson sent a letter to all Judges of the district courts in the state informing them that no prisoner would be confined at Granite who was over the age of 23 years, anyone who had been committed two or three offenses, or anyone who was sentenced for ten years. He said all such prisoners must be sent to McAlester. This was an important step in differentiating the role of a penitentiary. An important contribution of Warden George Waters was the training of inmates in scientific agriculture. He planned to start experimental seed farms and specialized in hogs, sheep, and cattle husbandry. When there was a new Governor, Warden Waters was terminated. Governor C. Walton had been elected in 1923, and there was much corruption at all levels which led to his impeachment. Some inmates received clemency even before they arrived at the reformatory. The inventories at some of the reformatory shops were ruthlessly plundered. Dr. Waters was reappointed as Warden "to clear up the mess." He then set the house in order again. Incompetent instructors were replaced by fine instructors from the bakery, kitchen, farm, tannery, and shoe shop. (When I went to work at OSR, they had just eliminated the shoe shop, which had made excellent boots and saddles.) In December 1925, there were 591 inmates who worked in plumbing, tinning, baking, cooking, tailoring, stone masonry, blacksmithing, carpentry, and tannery. Dr. Waters was very modest in all of his achievements. J.J. Savage, a later warden, reported in his annual report that all inmates were working, and there was no idleness. He said many of them were going to school half a day and were working half a day. He introduced an adequate wage system and wanted to transfer the prison to a "real reformatory."

In 1927, Mrs. George Waters became the Warden of OSR and carried on the work of her husband. She was the first and only female Warden of a large state reformatory for males. She became very popular locally and nationally. She focused mainly on religious and educational programs for inmates. In order to employ all prisoners, she leased several hundred acres of land. OSR already had 1400 acres of land in 1927. At the end of 1928, OSR's inmate population was 782, an increase of 176 prisoners in one year. Most criminals' offenses were property offenders, with 61 fowl thieves. There were two accidental deaths in 1928 from the rock crusher. The side of Wildcat Mountain was almost smooth then because inmates had manually "busted out" rocks on the mountain. Many inmates inscribed their names on the side of the mountain. (The name that I remember the most is "Chuck the Duck.") Many people today feel that inmates should still be chopping on the mountain for punishment. Mrs. Waters was one of the most convincing women speakers in the country. She was very enthusiastic about making OSR a model reformatory. She loved her "boys" who returned love and respect. (OSR inmates were mostly referred to as "boys.") She tried to make the prison their home. She believed religion was very important. While she was warden, there were hundreds of inmates baptized in the baptisteries outside the walls at OSR. Regardless of her efforts, some inmates mailed complaints to the authorities alleging cruel treatment by some staff members.

While there was an investigation proceeding against Warden Waters, there was a daring prison break at OSR. Prison riots, breaks, and protests were often characterized by unpredictability and other sudden course of developments. The prison staff was often unaware and unprepared. All of this was true of the prison break at OSR on February 17, 1935, soon after Sunday lunch. Thirty-one inmates made their bid for freedom during this daring escape. Eight of them surrendered in the front yard of the institution after being peppered with a blast from a shotgun by Deputy Warden M.T. Gallion. Two returned voluntarily and eighteen were at large until the following day. The inmates who initiated the break had somehow managed to smuggle two guns. They had threatened Officer Tom Denton and told him to unlock the prison doors. They later gunned down Peter Jones, the guard on the front tower. They gathered a number of women and children visitors in front of them, and they rushed the front steps. Getting in two cars in front of the prison, twenty of the men fled east. They later confiscated other cars and continued the flight. On Monday morning, they forced a housewife to make breakfast for them and a lunch to take with them. They then burglarized a house in Elk City, Oklahoma. When Mrs. Waters entered the prison, all of the doors were open and six officers were locked in the cells. She then approached the prison steps, and the inmates saw her. She got much encouragement as every hat went off to her. Her two sons, Victor Waters, county attorney of Greer

County and Dr. C.B. Waters, an intern at St. Anthony's Hospital in Oklahoma City, hurried to Granite to be available to their mother. Warden Water's son, Dr. C. B. Waters took care of the wounded prisoners. All of the Waters applied their skills to serve the reformatory "boys" in different ways. Mrs. Peter Jones, the slain guard's wife, also worked in the reformatory and saw her husband shot. All of the inmates liked her. She was known as "Mother" to them. Many of them helped her at her work in the guard kitchen, and the slain guard was known as "Uncle Pete." Evidently, there was an atmosphere of family before the break. Mrs. Waters was later fired and replaced by Sheriff Fred Hunt which ended the era of the Waters family at the reformatory.

The quarry operation continued until the mid-1940's. The prisoners working at the quarry operation had to drag the heavy ball and chains attached to their ankle. In addition, they had to carry a ten pound "double jack" sledgehammer over their shoulders. The crushed rock was sent to receiving points in the country. The railroad tracks extended inside the prison were used to transport prisoners and bring fuel oil for the boilers of the prison steam plant. The steam plant provided heat for the primary facility, warden's and deputy warden's residences, and provided raw steam for the kitchen, laundry, and electric generator room. The room under the main rotunda was a solitary confinement cell and still has an original steel plate door.

In 1985, all of the prisoners at OSR were moved to the new units on the yard. Most of them liked the old cell houses better because they could get a breeze through the bars. In the new units, there was not any ventilation and it was very hot until they installed air conditioning in the cells. OSR now had "A" Unit, "B" Unit, "C" Unit, and "D" Unit inside the walls; and "G" Unit, the Trustee Building, and a garment factory outside the walls. The garment factory was supervised by a small, elderly lady. She supervised about 200 inmates by herself. All of the inmates respected her, and they knew not to challenge her. There was an upholstery shop, but it had closed before I retired.

Now there are approximately 1,000 inmates who are housed at Oklahoma State Reformatory. They all are on the old side. In July 2012 the Department of Corrections removed every inmate there under the age of forty and sent them to other facilities in the state. They were replaced with offenders who were older. This move was made because of the violence that understaffed prison employees had to deal with.

This move appears to be working. In 2012 the medium-security prison in far western Oklahoma had thirty-five assaults and fifty cases of intentional injury.

Difficulty filling dozens of Correctional Officer and staff positions is part of the problem. Correctional Officers at OSR start making only $11 per hour. This is not very much money considering they put their lives on the line every day. Other people don't want to work there at the prison when they can get better paying jobs in oil fields. Also, they do not want to work at a prison known for physical assaults on Officers and inmates. Officers would come to work with thoughts of violence on their minds.

Since older inmates have been sent to the prison, only seven incidents of violence that were severe have been recorded.

There has been an increase in hiring Correctional employees during the last year. However, there are still two dozen empty Correctional Officer positions.

Basically the older inmates just mingle with other older inmates on the yard. The only Officers who can be seen are in the towers on the corners of the prison walls

The Warden wants more Correctional Officers on the yard after the switch to older inmates. Now he feels safe with the inmates interacting with each other. He said violence has almost been eliminated. The Warden also does not have to worry what is going to happen next. He said that the older inmates seem to be calmer and less inclined toward violence than the younger inmates who had been there. Most of the Correctional Officers and staff agree with this explanation. A female employee who is in charge of the kitchen feels safe even though there is lack of Officers.

An inmate who is sixty-four years old, who is serving time on multiple robbery and fire arms charge, said that he has spent much time at several facilities in Oklahoma. He feels that OSR is the safest of them all. However, he does not think OSR has enough medical services.

The small medical Dispensary there also has trouble filling staff positions. The regular doctor there is Noble L. Ballard who is an excellent physician. There have been many doctors, nurses, and pharmacists who have helped me with allergic reactions to wasp stings. I was stung by seven or eight wasps at one time. I had to go there and get many anti-venom injections.

Some inmates who have severe ailments on conditions are forced to go to other hospitals at other facilities. There are more medical needs because of the switch to older prisoners. The monthly average for cardiovascular illnesses has increased more than eight hundred percent. Liver diseases have more than tripled. Actual medical visits at the Dispensary have more than doubled.

One of the biggest issues has been mental illness. In a two year period, inmates at OSR who had mental health needs or a history of mental illness, increased by almost forty-five percent.

There seems to be an aging trend at the state's prisons. Now twenty percent of the state's prisoners are fifty and older compared to 5% in 1980. There are 4,484 inmates and that number will rise to 5,254 inmates in a few years. The expenses to care for inmates in the state prison system now totals in $59.4 million compared to $34.2 million in 2000.

From the outside, OSR hasn't changed much. The front tower and granite façade seems tireless and unchanging. However, inside is a modern facility trying to achieve the vision of Kate Barnard. She said, "The time has come when a modern system should be adopted for the State Penitentiary at McAlester and the Reformatory at Granite. A system should be devised which reforms criminals and prevents future crime."

Currently, Oklahoma prisons are filled to capacity. The agency is seeking $6.4 million in supplemental appropriation. Only 11% of Oklahoma inmates up for parole get approved for release. This cost taxpayers an average of $80 million per year. The parole board has the final say in the process, and the governor has the final say in the process of those convicted of violent crimes. Oklahoma has nearly 1,700 offenders in county jails awaiting transportation to the Corrections Department when beds become available. The Department continues to struggle to hire and retain enough staff to manage its prison population.

Other than the financial dilemma, the Corrections Department is also facing a problem with the smuggling and using of cell phones in all Oklahoma prisons. They are usually smuggled into the visiting room. Officers find many of them in shake-downs. Inmates can communicate to others inmates in their own prison or other prisons to coordinate escapes. Now their calls can be monitored by prison officials. Some states such as Texas and California have developed specials systems to intercept cell phone use. Oklahoma is also trying to do so.

Nevertheless, my co-workers and I provided recreation in the gym seven days a week for twenty-three years. Since we have retired, there is a gym supervisor and one assistant. The gym is open during the week and is closed on weekends. I miss providing recreational activities for the inmates, but I don't miss the stress.

Oklahoma State Reformatory from the northeast corner of the facility.

We knew where we were when we were entering the prison.

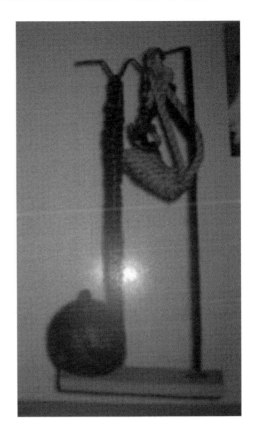

Ball and chain which was used by inmates while chopping on Wildcat Mountain so they would not escape

A Granite rock which was cut from Wildcat Mountain

Kate Barnard, the first Commissioner of Charities and Corrections

MICHAEL A. NORCROSS

Chapter 2
RECREATION IS REHABILITATION

When I went to work at the Oklahoma State Reformatory as a Recreation Supervisor, I did not know what to expect. I was a little apprehensive when I walked into the facility, and the iron gate closed behind me. I knew that I would not be able to exit unless an officer operating the gate would allow me to leave. The trustees gave me many inquisitive looks. I gave them many inquisitive looks, also. I wondered what I was doing working in a prison. Dannie Blevins and I walked into the prison at the same time and were met by David Morris, who was the Training Officer. Because of him, we immediately had a positive impression of OSR because he was so nice and was so likeable. He was our trainer for about a month and he was excellent. He had coffee brewed every morning before our training session, and he couldn't have done better. Once a year at OSR, we would have training sessions in CPR, first aid, and self-defense. Part of his training was about write-ups. In 23 years of working, I only wrote up about 6 inmates. I learned that a write-up can sometimes do more damage than good. I tried informally to solve the problem with an inmate instead of writing him up.

After a month of training with Dave, Dannie and I went for three weeks to Taft, Oklahoma, to the Training Academy. After the training was over, four of us took a DOC car to return to Granite. Two employees sat in the front, and another employee and I sat in the back. The car was made to transport inmates in the back seat. There was a steel mesh separating the front and back seats and no door handles, so the inmates could not escape. There was no way to obtain entrance from the back seat to the front. In case of a rollover or fire, the backseat passengers were in grave danger of burning to death. Luckily we safely made the return to Granite.

I had a college degree in Recreational Leadership/Recreation Therapy, and there were not many state jobs in that field. Two other Recreational Supervisors and I were hired to provide sports and tournaments for the inmates. This was very important in a prison because there is so much leisure time. I always thought that inmates were sent to prison for punishment, but I learned that the purpose of incarceration was rehabilitation. Our recreation programs were developed to rehabilitate inmates. My co-workers and I were not always successful. From the day that we walked into the prison, we did not have ample time to tarry because we immediately had to develop a summer softball schedule for the inmates. From then and for the rest of our careers at OSR as Recreation Supervisors, we tried to enhance the concept that the purpose of incarceration in a prison was rehabilitation, not punishment. We tried to rehabilitate inmates through recreation, so once released from prison, they would become productive citizens.

These are two examples of specific inmates and their rehabilitation at OSR through recreation:

I personally read Wiley Post's original record card at OSR. He was probably the most famous inmate at OSR. He was a world traveled aviator.

He later died in a plane crash in Alaska. He was in prison for robbery but was soon paroled and pardoned because of his leadership while playing on the prison baseball team; thus they felt that he had been rehabilitated. (Baseball was the only sport at OSR at that time. Recreation had not become an adjoining field yet.)

Another example is a person who was roommate in college with a friend of mine. My friend said that he was the nicest guy in college. Later, he became a basketball coach at a small town in Oklahoma. He was convicted and sent to OSR for killing his wife with a baseball bat. I knew the man who was the Town Marshall then, and he personally saw the pictures of that gruesome murder. He became the inmate "doctor" and did all of the surgical procedures on the inmates even though he had never been to medical school. He was also a very good basketball and softball player and was a captain whenever those teams traveled. (Those teams traveled with the inmates unchained. That later changed.) He was later discharged from prison and thought to be rehabilitated through recreational and sports activities. He left with the Maintenance Supervisor's wife and went to medical school in Florida with the agreement that he would never return to Oklahoma again.

After I had worked at OSR about 20 years, DOC sent me to a meeting of the National Correction Recreation Association in Fresno, California. This was completely paid for me and my wife went at her own expense. Every day for a week I went to recreation workshops pertaining to correctional recreation. The most interesting workshop was

"Growing Therapy." This was about how growing plants can be therapeutic to inmates. The purpose of these workshops was how I could help rehabilitate inmates through these activities. I tried to apply what I learned to the inmates when I got back to prison in order to help in their rehabilitation.

The front cover of the workbook at the National Correctional Recreation Association meeting in Fresno, California

> owing Experience - Therapeutic Use of Horticulture
> **Objectives and Workshop Content:** Participants will
> horticulture therapy and its relationship to rehabilitation.
> increase their understanding of the role of horticulture in
> recreational, social and substance abuse program compo
> **About the Presenter:** Karen Markland has been a Rec
> the past 10 years and has been employed by the Fresno
> Department for the last 9 years, where she works in an i
> setting She is an Active Master Gardener through the Un
> Extension.

"Growing Therapy" was my favorite workshop that I attended.

Chapter 3
MY CO-WORKERS-MY FRIENDS

I began working at OSR on February 1, 1984. My co-worker, Dannie Blevins started working the same day that I did, and he retired from there about a year after I did. He also had a degree in Recreational Leadership. Bobby Craft, our supervisor, had a degree in Physical Education and taught school for one year. He had come to work about a year before Dannie and me, and he retired about the same year as Dannie. Our titles were Recreation Supervisors and Bobby's title was Recreation Program Supervisor. Wayne Braun worked with Bobby before Dannie and I were hired, but he did not have a college degree. Therefore, he had to relinquish his job and become fulltime security. Even though we had official titles, the inmates always called us "coach." Some inmates called me "Mikey" which was a name I did not particular like. My mother even made a sweatshirt for me with "Coach" sewn on the front with a real whistle hanging down. However, I never wore it to work. All three of us always wore street clothes and officers wore uniforms. Our titles were later changed to Correctional Activities Officers and Correctional Activities Supervisor. None of us liked the latter titles; therefore, we called ourselves by our first titles. None of us had an abundance of confidence when we first started, and inmates noticed this. However, we gained more confidence the longer that we worked there. The three of us made a good team. Bobby was good in public relations, Dannie was good in security, and I was good at paper work, even though all of us had to rotate in the other areas. Many times all three of us would have to put keys at the front door, help in the kitchen, take inmates to the canteen, and shake inmates down. These duties were in addition to our recreational duties. Dannie was probably stricter on the inmates than Bobby and I, but he had a heart of gold. Bobby always supported me in everything I did. I will always be eternally grateful to him for that.

We provided all of the sports, activities, and tournaments for the inmates. We all had different days off, but we provided our recreational services seven days a week. We had leagues in softball, basketball, and volleyball. Softball was the most popular. We had many tournaments in the gym. Pool tournaments were the most popular. All three of us were friends at work and nothing ever happened to harm that friendship while we worked together. However, because of the ongoing stress in prison, we did occasionally "get on each other's nerves." Sometimes I was under much stress. Because of this, I would combatively confront an inmate, even though the inmate had not done anything. However, there was never a fight. I guess I just needed a relief of stress. All three of us have remained friends since retirement from Corrections. We all get together and talk about the good, bad, and humorous memories. We all knew the importance of treating inmates like "human beings." I guess they all liked us. They treated us as human beings too. The inmates had a newspaper called *Grapevine*. The first issue of it had a cartoon of the three of us on the cover.

Some of our most humorous memories happened to the three of us when two of us were together traveling in a car. Once, I was on my way home from Granite, and Dannie was driving just behind me. I noticed that he was making a motion with his arm for me to pull over on the side of the road. I thought that my engine was on fire. I pulled over on the side of the road. Dannie just drove on by me and waved.

Once, Dannie and I had gone to Stillwater, Oklahoma, for a training session. He had driven up there, and I had driven back. He always commented how slowly that I drove. He said that I would be passing a truck and I would pull in just before I hit the oncoming truck. The way that he would describe the sound of that passing truck was "Whoom."

There was a teacher at OSR by the name of Gary Hall, who had moved to Chickasha, Oklahoma, and gone to work at a facility near there. Bobby and I went to a meeting at Ouachita Correctional Center, which was on the Oklahoma-Arkansas line. We went to Chickasha to give Gary a ride. When we arrived early in the morning, he and his wife greeted us. We were getting ready to leave and his wife said, "Watch out! Gary's got a heavy foot." We didn't realize her meaning, but we soon found out. Gary drove to the Correctional Center. Gary was a great guy, but he drove fast all the way, even around curves. I was trying to sleep in the back seat, but obviously I couldn't. Bobby was sitting on the passenger side in the front seat. The entire trip I heard him constantly saying, "Slow this thing down!" It scared both of us. We went around one curve going so fast that it hit the guard rail. There was about a hundred foot drop off on the other side of the guard rail. I am sure that if we hadn't hit the guard rail, we would have dropped off in the canyon. When we got back to the institution, I don't know how we explained the dent on the side of the car. Whenever the three of us get together, we always talk about the ride with Gary Hall. That was the only time that I was so scared I felt my life was threatened.

    Since we all have been retired, Bobby is working at a golf course supervising work center inmates, and Dannie is working for home health taking care of elderly people.

Coach sweatshirt made by my mother. However I never wore it to work.

This cartoon is of three of us on the front cover of the inmates' newsletter *Grapevine*.

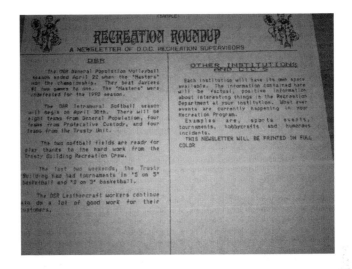

I tried to get a statewide newsletter for recreation supervisors, but it did not work out.

My former boss, Bobby Craft, in front of his new place of employment after he retired from DOC.

My former co-worker, Dannie Blevins, participating in his favorite sport after he retired from DOC.

MICHAEL A. NORCROSS

Chapter 4
MANY WARDENS, DEPUTY WARDENS, MAJORS – DIFFERENT PHILOSOPHIES

While I worked at OSR, I worked under many Wardens, Deputy Wardens, and Majors. The Warden was the chief official at a prison. There were usually two Deputy Wardens who were under his supervision. One of the Deputy Wardens supervised security, and the other Deputy Warden supervised programs. The Major was the Chief of Security. I knew several during my employment and was familiar with their philosophies that affected their demeanor on the job.

Jerry Sunderland was the first warden of my employment and was probably the strictest. He was employed there a long time. He was "employee-oriented." He once told me that security was too relaxed in the gym; therefore, I should be wary. After he retired from Corrections, he went to work for the Oklahoma State Bureau of Investigation. The Warden prior to Sunderland was John Grider who was Warden for about seven years before my employment at OSR. Hal, his brother, was an Assistant District Attorney and Tony, his son, helped me with recreation when we both worked for Court-Related and Community Services under the Department of Human Services.

David Miller was another Warden who was intelligent and progressive. He cared about employees and inmates. I will always be grateful to him because there were two escapes under my watch on the softball field. I could have gotten fired, but he prevented that and was lenient. He told me that I was a "good employee." He supported our recreation programs and was instrumental in implementing soccer, which became a popular sport.

Warden Steve Hargett oversaw the constructions of new guard houses on the corners of the walls and emphasized cleanliness of the institution. We kept the gym immaculate. Cigarette butts or trash on the yard was never an issue. He seemed to be prouder of the trophies that we won at softball and basketball tournaments than any other Warden.

One Warden who came to OSR had been the Warden at a minimum security prison. He tried to transform OSR from a high medium-low maximum facility into a minimum facility. Unfortunately, this proved disastrous. He wanted to start a salad bar at the chow hall; it failed. He eliminated the fences, which separated the protection and general population. This troubled all of the employees. He assured us that "Hell is not going to break loose." Hell did break loose though. After this, many protective custody inmates were killed. He was an inmate-oriented Warden; therefore, most of the inmates liked him. Most employees did not.

There was a sweet lady who was the Deputy Warden's secretary that sometimes did the typing for the recreation department. I was in her office one day and happened to look down on her desk. On it were letters headed, "Let's have a party!" This particular Warden was mailing them to legislators, DOC officials, and former employees. The "party" started in the gym about two weeks later with no air-conditioning in the middle of August. There were about two hundred people in the gym making it unbearably hot. We had a band on a raised platform. Suddenly, the warden jumped on the stage and said, "Let's start the party!" The band commenced. The crowd was in awe of this fiasco. However, several months later when an inmate was killed violently in the gym and I became upset, he supported me and sent a nurse to assist me.

Warden L. L. Young was a nice likeable Warden, but unfortunately, he was the Warden when an employee was killed while he was warden. He had to deal with the after math of that tragedy.

The Warden when I retired from OSR was Eric Franklin. He was an effective Warden and supported all of our recreation programs at the prison.

A note of interest was about a prior warden who worked at OSR from 1949 to 1969. Everyone said that Joe Harp was a great Warden. He was instrumental in implementing Lakeside School in 1947. It was the first accredited high school inside prison walls in the United States. Starting in 1949, it was the first racially integrated school in the state. An Officer who worked under him said that he was a tough Warden. The inmates respected him.

The Deputy Warden who worked under Jerry Sunderland was Sam Cook. He worked at OSR for forty-two years, beginning as a farm supervisor for the inmates who worked in the fields picking cotton and other crops. (After retirement, he started playing a guitar in a country band.) He said that after inmates would work all day picking cotton they were so tired that their only interest was returning to the cell house, taking a shower, and going to bed. He said this certainly eliminated trouble or riots. Of course, many human rights organizations have since banned inmates picking cotton. They feel it is too demeaning. Such organizations have gone so far as to label the inmates as "clients."

The Deputy Warden under David Miller was Arnold Waggoner, a very innovative supervisor. He encouraged tournaments and even awarded soft drinks as prizes. He arranged many banquets in the gym. One was in honor of Larry Meachum, the then Director for the Department of Corrections. When he got up to speak, all of the inmates gave him a standing ovation in the gym. We had never been able to play softball at night because we lacked lights. Deputy Warden Waggoner solved that issue. The inmates always appreciated what he did to reduce stress.

Larry Hahn was a good program-oriented Deputy Warden and always supported our recreation programs. He was originally employed as a Correctional Officer but was promoted through the ranks. He was well liked by staff and inmates.

Randy Parker was a very efficient, effective, and likeable Deputy Warden who supervised the gym about two years. He cared about staff and inmates. He was an enjoyable boss and knew how to deal with people. He had enough confidence in us that he allowed us to conduct our recreation programs the way we wanted. We respected and loved the man.

Ken Klingler began as a Deputy Warden, was promoted to Warden, and then eventually to DOC

Headquarters. He must have been sharp and intelligent.

The Deputy Warden who first interviewed me for Recreation Program Supervisor was Mike Watkins. I did not get that job because I did not have a teaching certificate. Bobby got the job because he had a teaching certificate, and I later became his assistant.

There was a Deputy Warden who was always pressuring us. He would get angry whenever we incorrectly filed any incident report. When an inmate was written up, the paper work would go the Unit Manager first; then it went to the Deputy Warden. This Unit Manager would intercept the incident report and correct it before it went to the Deputy Warden in order to protect us.

The first Major at OSR when I worked there was Lawrence Mitchell. He was well-liked and respected. He was there for only a few months when I arrived. I heard him make the statement once about inmates in the gym. He said eight inmates were too many to be in the gym with one employee by himself. What would he have said to one hundred fifty inmates in the gym with one employee?

Gaylord Inks was promoted through the ranks to Major. He was well-liked as a Chief of Security. All of the Correctional Officers, Sergeants, Lieutenants, and Captains respected and supported him. He was the so called "judge" when an inmate was "written up" for some offense. He decided on an inmate's punishment. The employee represented the inmate in the manner that a lawyer would in court. He later transferred to another facility as a Deputy Warden.

After Gaylord, there came another Major who was disliked by most employees and inmates, except for one Captain who felt he was efficient. I never heard a good thing about him. He went into the barber shop one time and our barber, Archie Nichols, told him, "Get your ass out of here and don't come back." He didn't. He was extremely over weight; the inmates jeered him and talked about his big ass. He and his wife were caught burglarizing the Warden's home and was fired. (Speaking of the barber shop, at one time inmates were allowed to cut employee's hair. However, they had to have permission from Archie to use any kind of after shave lotion that contained alcohol.)

RECREATION FROM BEHIND PRISON WALLS

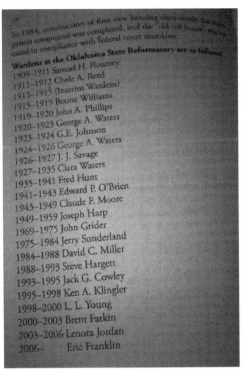

Total number of Wardens at OSR. There have been several Wardens since Eric Franklin.

Clara Waters, the first female warden in a male prison in the United States

Joseph Harp was warden at OSR for 20 years. When he told inmates to clear the yard, they better clear the yard!

Chapter 5
THE OLD GYM – OUR PLAYGROUND

The three of us worked in an old gym that was built in the 1950's and was not air-conditioned. At one time the painted, wooden floor was in excellent condition, but the roof leaked. It completely warped the floor. To remedy this, the whole floor was cemented, which prevented a basketball from bouncing as it should. This upset many inmates. We did have glass backboards at the end of the court and had four metal backboards running from the sides so that two games could be played at once. Many basketball and volleyball games were played in the gym. We had a volleyball net held by poles cemented on tires. We had a volleyball league which followed the basketball league. The best intramural basketball was "Show Time." Volleyball was not as popular as basketball. We had one wall painted for hand ball lines. We had a broken window next to the hand ball lines. Many times the hand ball would go through the window. We then would have to go outside and retrieve the ball. We had two ping pong tables in the area next to the basketball court. We also had a boxing bag and two stationary bicycles at the edge of the basketball court. The inmate, who used the boxing bag, was an inmate named Hot Dog. His nickname was aptly fitting because of his aggressiveness. The boxing bag got broken many times and had to be repaired.

In a room away from the basketball court, we had four pool tables. Many pool tournaments were played on these tables. There also was a "cage" to keep supplies. At one time the cage was used as a projector room to show movies on Saturdays and Sundays. The showing of movies had ended right after I came to work there because most inmates had televisions. (The fact that inmates had their own televisions was a cause of anger from many employees and the general public.) All TV's were on cable. Paul Everhart worked in electronics and was on call 24 hours a day to fix the cables. Paul was also a Corrections Professor at Western Oklahoma State College in Altus.

    The room next to the pool room was our office. The office did not have any windows, but after an inmate was killed in the gym, windows were installed so that the gym area could be better observed. The room next to our office was a room for leather craft workers. One of our leather craft workers was Floyd Vinson, who was in prison for cattle rustling, but was an excellent saddle maker. He knew Reba McIntire and made a saddle for her. She sent him a personal thank you card. The leather craft room had previously been used for weight-lifting and weight-lifting tournaments. Mike Swanson was usually the inmate who helped us with the tournaments. Lights for the gym floor hung down from the ceiling and were about twenty feet from the gym floor. We had a special device used to change the light bulbs. When inmates were allowed to smoke in the gym, we had cans around the walls for cigarette butts, but this was eliminated when smoking was banned at the prison. There were big bleachers on the north side of the gym with opening windows above them. The gym was so secure that if we were ever taken hostage, a blow torch would be needed to cut in there. Our gym crew did an excellent job of cleaning for inspections before and after activities.

When we first started working in the gym, there were six to eight officers responsible for the gym. When a new warden arrived, we were required to keep the gym open seven days a week by ourselves. We had general population inmates five nights a week and protective custody inmates two nights a week at different times. When Protective Custody was in the gym, we had to keep a chain on the door. This was done in order to keep out the General Population inmates. Once, I forgot to latch the chain. However, I remembered before the inmates got there.

The heat! You can imagine the heat in a gym full of active men with no air-conditioning in the summer time. At times it was unbearable. On the other hand, the gym was extremely cold in the winter. We had only six heaters that hung from the ceiling. Once, in the middle of winter on a Saturday night, I forgot to turn on the heaters. Dannie came to work on Sunday, and it was freezing. Oh, that made him angry!

Outside of the gym were a basketball goal, a volleyball court, and two horseshoe pits. The volleyballs would often get cut by the razor wire. I would take them home and patch them. When I first came to work, there was a boxing ring on the yard which had been used for inmates who had a "bone" to pick with each other. They would put boxing gloves on each of the inmates, and they would fight each other until they were tired and had their problem solved. They took the ring down shortly after I came to work there. It seemed that boxing would be a better way to amend differences than to stick a shank in each other. They also played handball on the outside of the gym wall.

We put up a net and tried to spark interest in tennis. Walt Pierce, an inmate, tried to initiate this interest among other inmates. However, we had to eliminate tennis because the balls kept going over the wall.

One lady Deputy Warden always wanted us to have pizza parties in the gym. The inmates filled out the proper paper work to buy the pizzas. We took the orders to Pizza Hut, and they delivered the pizzas to the prison. On the night they delivered the pizzas, the inmates came to the gym one unit at a time. The names of the inmates and the type of pizza were called. The inmates got their pizzas from our office. Before we started distributing the pizza, an inmate hid the list of the inmates' order, but we found it in the trash can and continued with the party. Each unit that we had in the gym usually numbered over 100 inmates, and not once was there a mistake in the pizza orders. We had several participate in these pizza parties. The inmates acted like they enjoyed and appreciated the effort we had made on the pizza parties. It made better employee-inmate relations.

The Highway Patrol Training Academy was in Burns Flat, Oklahoma. Many times, the cadets would have their training in the gym. Sometimes there would be 100 cadets in the gym.

In 1965 when I went to Altus Junior College, we played a basketball team at OSR. The bleachers were full of inmates. They naturally rooted for the inmate team. It scared all of us players. Nineteen years later, I had to make a living in the same gym as a Recreation Supervisor. I had to somewhat eliminate that fear in order to work there.

In 1982 I worked for CR&CS in Altus, Oklahoma. The Assistant District Attorney went with a basketball team to play a game at the OSR gym. The inmate who was refereeing the game had been convicted and sent there by him. He always thought that was funny.

Yes, there were many activities in the Old Gym – Our Playground.

My boss, Bobby Craft, in our office in the gym.

Chapter 6
THE BAND – MUSICAL CREATIVITY

At OSR, we had an upstairs room in the gym used exclusively for inmates to practice and play instruments. We had many bands at OSR who played mainly rock and country music. Most band players knew how to play when they came into prison while others learned there. One inmate told me that when he was in the county jail he learned the notes on the bass guitar from listening to the radio. When he came to prison, he was able to play the bass guitar. Our equipment included two guitars, a bass, a keyboard, and a drum set. The inmates who wanted to play an instrument were willing to practice and learn how to play it. Whenever strings were broken on the guitars or a drum skin was broken, we had the appropriations in our budget to replace them.

The "Rock Busters" was probably the most popular band. Before I came to OSR, bands were allowed to travel and perform, but that had ended before I arrived. The Rock Busters played many times at the amphitheater at Quartz Mountain State Lodge, and I went to hear them several times. The administration eventually had to stop them from playing outside the prison because the inmates were interacting with their families. Many times during certain holidays, inmate bands performed on the yard to the delight of inmates and staff.

One of the General Population (GP) rock bands favorite songs was "Route 66." Part of song read Flagstaff, Arizona; but they would always sing Phoenix, Arizona. I always corrected them; they found it funny. The same band was playing one night when Dannie smelled pot and cleared the room. We did have problems when general population and protective custody used the facility at separate times. GP used the room three nights a week and weekends; Protective Custody used it two nights a week. They both accused each other of abusing the equipment. The general population especially accused the protective custody inmates because GP always judged PC and called them "rats." The GP always played a variety of songs, and PC played very few songs. We kept a lock on the door. When we went into the room, we had to take the lock in there with us because they could lock us in there.

   On the negative side, one inmate who was on our gym crew donated guitar strings to the band program wanted the title "band coordinator." When he was not granted the title, he went to the band room and literally jerked the strings off the guitars. That was a stressful moment. When he cursed me, that was a stressful moment also. It was a stressful moment for him when I wrote him for disciplinary action. One of my co-workers said, "We didn't have a hair on our nut sack if we didn't fire the son of a bitch." We did fire him.

   My son, who was a good guitar player, and Ken Knight, an inmate on the gym crew, practiced in the gym room. Ken was a self-taught bass player and was the inmate in charge of our band program. He always did an excellent job. Soon after their practice together, inmate and civilian practice was no longer allowed in the prison anymore. My son said he felt a little uneasy playing with an inmate in a small room anyway, but he still had fun.

Generally, playing instruments in a band was a creative expression and an important way of reducing stress. It also was a learning experience useful in society. In one instance, I knew of an inmate who was released from prison and made a good living playing professionally in a band.

Oklahoma State Reformatory band with Clara Waters (right).

They marched in the first OSP rodeo in 1940.

Chapter 7

THE SOFTBALL FIELD - TEMPORARY RELIEF FROM STRESS

We had two softball fields outside the walls. The general population played there during the week and the minimum security on weekends; the protective custody inmates did not play there at all, except when soccer was implemented by the warden. They were the only classification of inmates that played there. We did not have soccer very long because it was difficult to play, and the inmates tired too easily. Softball was always our most popular sport. We had many games and tournaments there.

Joseph Harp Correctional Center, James Crabtree Correctional Center, and Dick Conner Correctional Center came for a tournament one day. I believe it was won by Joseph Harp Correctional Center. Trophies were given for first, second, and third places. A most valuable player award was given also. Going outside the walls to play softball was a tremendous relief of stress. We held games and tournaments on those fields for twenty years. When we counted the inmates going out of the walls, one could almost feel the stress lifted. When we counted the inmates coming back inside the walls, the stress increased. To ensure an accurate count, one Recreation Supervisor held one inmate unseen until the other Supervisor made count. This kept everyone alert and honest.

Security was always the biggest concern with inmates. First of all, we were outside with these inmates; then add aluminum bats to the mix. An inmate once told me privately that if fighting were to ensue to notify security as soon as possible. Luckily, nothing ever happened except for a few fist fights. There was an Officer with a gun on a tower in between the fields. He only had to use his gun once in twenty years. One time a batter and an umpire got into a fist fight because the batter thought that the umpire was making bad calls. Another time an umpire named Bobby Porterfield, who was on our gym crew and was highly liked and respected on the yard, was umpiring a game from behind the plate and called the batter out on strikes. The batter went to the bleachers and called Bobby a "punk," which is the wrong term to use among inmates. A brawl followed. Bobby and three of Bobby's friends hit him. The batter looked like his face had been run through a sausage grinder. An Officer on the Tower popped a shell in the air that stopped the fight. The batter couldn't apologize to Bobby enough. I had a 1959 baseball card named Bob Porterfield. I showed that to Bobby, and he thought that was pretty neat. It always helped to have friends in prison in time of need!

There were many teams with many names; the "Outlaws" was the catchiest name. The Outlaws usually won the league because they had the best players. Some said it was because they got to use the "blue dot" softballs, which were the best. Home runs to right field had to go over the wall to be a home run. A player by the name of Pancho Grayson was continually hitting home runs over the right field wall. We would gather up the balls inside the walls after the games. Balls hit to left field had to be legged out for a home run. This was on the east field. On the west field, the ball had to be hit over the left field wall for a home run. Balls hit out to right field had to be legged out for a home run.

One time an inmate escaped on the ball field. After that, when the inmates were brought back inside the walls for count, we had to check the dug outs and trash cans to ensure that there were no inmates hiding. We also had to count the inmates every 15 minutes while we were on the ball field.

An inmate once asked me to bring a six pack of tall boy Coors and put them in trash can. I told him that he was crazy. Employees cannot do that. He must have thought I was pretty stupid. He was discharged later. I am sure he drank a lot of beer then!

After the lights were fixed on the ball field, there were two all-star teams who played each other. Bobby, Dannie, and I were the umpires. A particular inmate, who was playing left field, began having severe muscle spasms and the medical staff was called. He had to be taken to the Dispensary for treatment.

I always wanted to line up the umpires before the games to make sure that we had them ready for the game. Bobby and Dannie would always tease me about that as they felt it unnecessary. Many times, though, my preplanning made the games go much smoother.

At the Trustee Building, Dannie coached the all-star team on Saturdays (even though the all-star team did not travel.) I had the regular league on Sundays. We usually had four teams in the league.

We played on the east field. We had league play the entire summer and about the last two weeks we had the play-offs. Soft drinks were given to the winning teams. The lights were not operable at the ball fields, so I had to make the inmates finish before sundown. If the games were not finished by then, we had a security problem. The Tower Officer could not see them as they walked back to their units.

Of all of the experiences that I had at OSR, I had more fond memories from the softball fields. Inmates really took their softball seriously. After about twenty years, a new housing unit and factory replaced the ball fields. Thus, our softball program ended. It was sad to see such a popular sport come to an end. Hence, some of the relief from stress was eliminated. What a shame!

My 1959 baseball card of Bob Porterfield. It had the same name as Bobby Porterfield, one of our favorite gym crew members

MICHAEL A. NORCROSS

Chapter 8
ALL-STAR TEAMS- WHAT A HASSLE!

As stated previously, the three main sports at OSR were softball, basketball, and volleyball. We picked all-star teams in softball and basketball, according to the inmates' talent. We usually picked fifteen players in softball and ten players in basketball to be all-stars. We picked all-star softball teams according to hitting and fielding ability, as well as attitude. Our basketball teams were picked according to shooting ability and defense. Attitude on all-star teams were very important. After the all-star teams were picked for basketball, we had basketball tournaments in the gym. Teams would come from other institutions, and we went to other institutions for tournaments. When we conducted our own tournaments, our teams wore uniforms and the referees wore striped shirts. An inmate ran the clock. Trophies were given for first, second, and third place, as well as the Most Valuable Player.

We won at least one basketball tournament at Joe Harp Correctional Center. We had a basketball player named Oscar Kirklin who could have easily played in college if not for his incarceration. He was our best basketball player. What a shame! A few players could have played baseball in college, notably "Pancho" Grayson, a great left-handed hitter.

We had many tournaments with other institutions at the softball fields. Once we were supposed to have a team from Altus Air Force play the All Star team, but we did not have enough security on the ball field. I had to call the Air Force team and tell them they could not come. Both teams were disappointed. An inmate from Carnegie, Oklahoma, was always worrying me about having a fast pitch tournament. I had to keep telling him no because we were concerned about injuries from the fast pitches.

Before a person on the street could come to a softball game, he would have to have prior approval. Once a lady came from far away and did not have that approval. We had no choice but disallow her entrance. However, she was not upset.

Once we were getting ready to have our all-star basketball teams play in the finals. I was going to supervise it on Saturday and Dannie on Sunday. Since these were finals, everyone was highly anxious. It had snowed on Friday, and I was unable to get my car out of the driveway. I had to call Dannie to take over the games, but he took it well.

We had trophies for all of the winners. One of our inmates picked for our all-star softball was nicknamed "rabbit" because of his protruding teeth. Another inmate who didn't make the team and thought that he should have said, "Did you just pick a rabbit out of a hat?"

We also went to other institutions for softball tournaments. They usually picked first, second, and third place, as well as a Most Valuable Player. At Crabtree Correctional Center we won the softball tournament. One of our players got MVP. Another player was upset because he thought that he should have gotten the award. The rest of the softball players got so tired of hearing his complaints all the way back to OSR.

In the gym, when our basketball all-star team would play another good team, the intensity was so great that there were a few fights with some of the players. I noticed that inmates usually bonded together like friends after they would fight. I had no choice but to "write them up." This was something that I hated to do. Once I picked an all-star team, we practiced for about a month and then planned to play in a basketball tournament. The team worked out to try to get ready for the tournament. They ran laps in the gym and up and down the steps on the bleachers. When they ran, I was running right along with them. I must have been in good shape. The day that we were supposed to go, the administration denied our trip. Imagine the incredible let down for the inmates. The inmate who was helping me coach the team thought it was my fault and chewed me out. I guess he needed a scapegoat.

It was great to have all-star teams because of the talent represented on a team. The difficulty in picking these teams was choosing the all-stars; all of them considered themselves worthy. However, we did our best, regardless of the criticism from those not chosen. It was a constant hassle picking all-star teams.

MICHAEL A. NORCROSS

Chapter 9
TRIPS TO BASKETBALL AND SOFTBALL TOURNAMENTS

Even though it was difficult to pick all-star teams in basketball and softball, we had fun when we traveled to different institutions to play softball and basketball. More than anything, it was a chance for the inmates to "escape" from the prison for a while, and the recreation provided temporary relief from stress. Staff also appreciated the respite. The misery for the inmates was chaining their wrists and ankles for the duration of the trip.

Many years ago, inmates were not chained going to sporting events. Crow Christian was the coach then. They went as far as Wichita Falls, Texas, to boxing matches without chains. They never had an incident or an inmate escape. The coach that came after Crow was Mack Dillahunty. We came after Mack.

When I worked at OSR and we traveled to other institutions, all of the inmates rode in one vehicle with a staff driver. The recreation staff would follow in another vehicle with all of the equipment. We once started to leave, got a short way down the road, and realized that we had left all of the softball equipment at the front tower. We had to hustle back and get it before the inmates' car got too far down the road.

Usually the Officer who drove the inmate vehicle was "Race Horse" Williams who was an excellent driver especially through Oklahoma City and Tulsa. He never had a wreck. Occasionally, we would get to eat at the host facility's cafeteria, but sometimes we would bring our own sandwiches and soft drinks.

When the inmates had to go to the rest room, like everyone else, we would stop at a gas station. We would escort them into the restroom with their chains attached. Customers and employees really gave them some cautious looks. Luckily, no one escaped. All of the inmates knew that if there was ever an escape or an incident, we would probably never be able to travel again. They didn't want that to happen.

What I remember about the Crabtree tournament was the recreation staff wasn't allowed on the field. We were separated by a chain link fence, so I would throw the soda we had brought for them over the chain link fence. I remember a certain inmate led us in prayer at the Joseph Harp basketball tournament. We won the tournament and this inmate got MVP; his prayer must have worked. He could have easily played college basketball. He told me that he regretted going to prison and missing the thrill of playing at the collegiate level. We usually had inmates coach in basketball because they knew so much more about the game than we did. At that tournament, fourteen of the fifteen players got to play. We forgot about the other player. The resentment showed on his face after the game. In the stands we saw many inmates who used to be inmates at OSR. We talked to a few of them.

We once went to a basketball tournament at Mack Allford Correctional Center. All of the players were fired up because they thought they would win it. We had a good enough team to win it. We took fifteen players out of sixteen potential players. The one player who we did not select to go said that we "played him like a rubber ball." When our basketball team walked down the side walk in the front of the prison, it was obvious that we were going to a sporting event. A cantankerous old man, who worked in maintenance, saw us filing past. He said that inmates should not be allowed to travel and compete in tournaments. He ranted about calling the Governor to get this entertainment stopped.

The Mack Allford tournament was a double elimination tournament. We got beat the first game by one point. Oscar Kirklin, a teammate, played a fantastic game and kept us in the game, but to no avail. That loss kind of took the "wind out of their sails." We lost the next game by a wide margin. One of our basketball players, who was doing a life sentence for murder, was a good basketball player, but was upset at the recreation staff referees. We had a hard time controlling him.

Of all the time that I worked as a Recreation Supervisor at OSR, I got the most satisfaction and had the most fun going to softball and basketball tournaments, whether we won or lost.

MICHAEL A. NORCROSS

Chapter 10
THE RODEO –MONEY THE HARD WAY

In 1940 when America was still at peace but the war had spread in Europe, an idea developed to hold a rodeo behind the walls of the Oklahoma State Penitentiary. Inmates and professional rodeo riders participated. The general public gathered behind the heavily-guarded walls of "Big Mac" to enjoy the show. The first announcement of the rodeo came in the September 30, 1940 issue of the McAlester newspaper. It told about "The Oklahoma State Penitentiary's First Annual Rodeo, the Biggest behind the Walls' Rodeo in the World." Warden Jess Dunn was called the "guiding light" of the program. He was inspired by an annual prison rodeo in Huntsville, Texas, which drew 30,000 visitors in 1940. This issue advertised that one hundred wild Mexican Brahman bulls and other rodeo stock had been engaged for the participation of many convicts who had previous rodeo experience. Inmates constructed stands on an eight acre plot just inside the walls. It seated up to 15,000 spectators. Tommy French, a lifer, served as the arena director. A parade kicked off the big event. The newspaper reported that the parade was "the most colorful" local event in the past decade. Four marching bands, including the McAlester High School marching band, participated along with floats and mounted entries. The Granite State Penitentiary marching band performed, but the McAlester prison band did not. The newspaper said that the McAlester prison's famous string band performed. The newspaper reported that prison officials had taken precautions to keep the inmates inside the walls of the maximum security facility while patrons could still enjoy the show. It read, "While the entire prison group is to witness the rodeo, there will be no contact at any time between the prisoners and the thousands of outside patrons." Prison officials said that the innovation of such entertainment was permitted to aid in the strengthening of the morale of the prison inmates.

Many OSR inmates traveled to the rodeo every year thereafter. It was a challenge to the inmates who participated in it. Even though I did not go with the inmates, I made the arrangements for them. We had other interested sponsors who would go with them each year. Several inmates placed on the events. Most excelled in bull riding. Many trophies were awarded and brought back to OSR awarded for their bull riding abilities. Even though the rodeo was always held at OSP at McAlester, I often thought that OSR had the facilities to accommodate a prison rodeo.

The annual Oklahoma State Prison Rodeo grew into an event attended by people across the nation. It became the subject of national magazine articles and was featured on national television programs. I remember one article in a local paper that captioned an inmate riding a bull. It declared, "Money, the Hard Way."

The front entrance to the OSP rodeo

Program for the rodeo which costs $0.25

Inmate riding bull- This event was OSR inmates' best event.

MICHAEL A. NORCROSS

Chapter 11
A MOVIE SIMILAR TO SPORTS AT OSR

The New Mexico Penitentiary erupted in a riot in 1980. Sometime after that, the prison was purchased by the New Mexico's Film Commission for continued film makers' use. In 2004, the film *The Longest Yard,* was remade at the prison. The prison is now used as a tourist attraction for tours. Tour guides take the public into the gas chamber and through death row. They emphasize the hatchet marks cut on the floor, where Paulina Paul's head was severed, or where a one-armed man almost lost the other arm to the blade of a biker who had gone crazy. Many believe there are ghosts in the prison. They groan in the darkness of the gas chamber or in the death row. They sound like wolves or like humans who have been wounded. It seems to worsen when cameras flash. The wailing can be heard by everyone. A guard, who worked there in 1980, played a security guard on the movie set. He told about the aftermath of the riot. He was working in a room which used to be the gas chamber. He also was assigned the job of photographing new inmates. A blurred inmate's face was produced in one of his photos. He took many pictures, but some got foggier until a face appeared. He took more pictures. The face got clearer, but eventually disappeared. He took the photo to the mental health department, but it showed nothing. He then brought the photo to a person in the records' department. She searched the microfilms and found a likeness of David Nelson Cooper, the only person to have been killed in the gas chamber.

The film *The Longest Yard* portrayed recreational activities very similar to those at OSR. The film enacted the importance of sports to inmates at both prisons. The movie was about football. We had flag football at one time, but it was discontinued because physical injuries because an issue. (There was an inmate at OSR named Arnie Reubke. His brother, Alex Van Pelt, played for the Pittsburgh Steelers football team. When Pittsburgh was playing in Dallas, he would sign autographs for the inmates and employees.) The movie depicted all of the inmates who played on the outside basketball courts; basketball on outside courts was very popular at OSR. In the movie, weight lifting was popular on the yard. At OSR, we had many outside weightlifting areas always in use. The football game played in the movie was at an arena with bleachers so that the public could watch the game. Armed guards were on duty in case of an escape. The setting of this game in the movie was similar to the Prison Rodeo at the Oklahoma State Penitentiary. Handball was popular at OSR and in the real prison. The prison in New Mexico was built about the same time as OSR. There are similarities in the architecture of the two.

The old prison, torn up by the riot, was closed November 21, 1998. They have since built new buildings around the old prison.

RECREATION FROM BEHIND PRISON WALLS

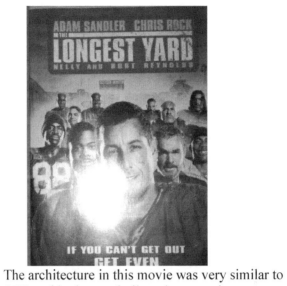

The architecture in this movie was very similar to OSR and both were built at the same time.

MICHAEL A. NORCROSS

Chapter 12
WE CAN TAKE YOU HOSTAGE ANYTIME

When my co-workers and I supervised the gym, we were usually assigned an average of one hundred fifty inmates a night. With that many inmates, you were basically "you" and they were "they." Most inmates realized this and gave their respect. It was obvious that inmates could take hostages or kill anytime. However, more inmates meant more "snitches," to tell on the others. Also, recreation was an extra-curricular activity which helped reduce stress; and the recreation was something that inmates enjoyed. As employees, we were trained in hostage situations. The best advice given from a training Officer was to cooperate with the inmates and don't "get the John Wayne" syndrome. Luckily, in working twenty-three years at OSR, I was never taken hostage. Neither of my co-workers was taken hostage either. I attribute my success to my interaction with the inmates; I treated them like "human beings" and never acted like I was superior to them. The first summer that I worked there I heard rumblings from inmates that there would be a riot that summer. That made me a little uneasy, but it never happened. I knew that I had to make a living, so I put everything in the hands of the Lord and everything worked out fine.

People noticed that I am religious, have high morals, and do not curse. Several times, I went downstairs to get a soda from the machine where others fellow workers assembled. One of the Officers saw me and said, "Here's Mike. Don't say anything nasty." I guess they respected me. Inmates have warned me that other inmates were "going to get me." Apparently some inmates respected me enough to protect me. Thankfully, I was never injured.

In order to get an accurate count sometimes, we had to "two-them-up." This meant two lines of inmates. We counted them as they filed by us. This was difficult to do because inmates don't like to be "two-ed up." Many times during gym hours, we would have to get a count by just going around and counting them while they participated in their activities. My co-worker Dannie Blevins once had over 250 inmates in the gym by himself and had to count them while they participated in the activities. You can imagine how difficult that was to get a count.

One night Officers failed to get a good count. Captain Sam Callens, who was a tough, likeable Captain, came to the gym to assist. The two of us managed the count of about one hundred of them. We didn't "two-them-up," but called their names from a previous count sheet. I pointed for individuals to go to a certain area of the gym. This was a tense situation because it was a show of force. They could have taken us hostage anytime! Sometime later, an inmate named "Doc" Coggins, who was well liked and respected on the yard asked, "When are ya'll going to count us like that again?" I guess our show of force displayed courage and had impressed him.

While I was at OSR, there was a large weightlifter who took a woman hostage in the library. It did not last very long as Officers trained in hostage-taking situations resolved the matter, and she was not injured.

We practiced a mock emergency hostage situation in the gym once. Bobby, Dannie, and I played the role of hostages. I pretended that I had diabetes, did not have insulin, and was going into diabetic shock. (Mike Miller, who was playing the role of the hostage-taker, took me seriously, but I told him that I was just pretending.) Therefore, he let me go. I then told the Warden, Deputy-Warden, and Major that the hostage-taker had stabbed one of my co-workers and had threatened to use the knife again. The CERT team Officers captured the hostage-taker. To create a realistic situation, prison officials called all of our spouses at work. My wife was a teacher at Lone Wolf Public Schools. It scared her to death until they told her it was a mock situation.

Many years before I came to work at OSR, there was a hostage situation in the kitchen. Paul Morris and his brother were used as snipers in the towers in the situation. Paul covered the back towers of the kitchen area where inmates were holding hostages. He had a scoped rifle and his view of the kitchen was the south area with an inmate acting as sentry. He prayed that he would not have to shoot anyone. The inmates inside the prison made certain demands of administrators and then proceeded to use the kitchen to cook and eat steaks. Paul and another Correctional Officer on the tower had not eaten since the day before. Paul said that lying on a concrete run looking through a scope was a challenge, but his concerns were the hostages in the kitchen. Someone finally tossed a couple of apples to them. The situation was finally resolved when the administration and the inmates came to an agreement, and no one was injured.

Another hostage incident occurred at OSR before I worked there. Teachers at the school were taken hostage for two days at the school. The hostages had planned an overall prison takeover to begin in the kitchen. However, their timing was off. The inmates put bags over the teachers' heads for the duration of the situation. The holding card was the Principal, Tom Warren. They held a knife to his throat. He told them that if they were going to cut his throat to go ahead and do it. Food for the inmates was sent in from the mess hall. After two days, Officers, who had been trained in hostage situations, resolved the takeover.

Chapter 13
ANY INMATE CAN GET KILLED

When any inmate comes into prison, he soon becomes aware that death is a common consequence for some actions. As employees, we know this and are careful what we say about an inmate because it can incriminate him. The most common way that an inmate can get killed is "snitching." A snitch is an inmate who tells an employee what another inmate has said or done. Another common way an inmate can get killed is getting into debt with another inmate. During the twenty-three years that I worked in the prison, there were many snitches who were killed.

I remember several incidents in which inmates were killed. One was a group of inmates who were supposed to be doing plumbing work in the basement of the prison. Actually, they were digging out under the wall in order to escape. During the digging, a trustee told security about the escape plan. Of course, the operation was stopped. The inmates were "written up." Everyone thought the situation had been resolved. The inmates, who were digging the tunnel, somehow discovered who had snitched on them. The next day, an employee named Greg Brooks, went into the bathroom in the basement and found the inmate who had snitched. He had his throat cut and a sign around his neck, which read *RAT*. Being a rat or a snitch was one of the worst labels that an inmate could be dubbed by other inmates. The inmates guilty of the murder were sent to the maximum security prison in McAlester.

In the gym one night, I was in my office making preparations to take our basketball team to a tournament the next day. An inmate came into the office and said, "You better get the first aid kit and go out to the gym area." I discovered that an inmate in the weight lifting area had been stabbed probably fifty times in the chest area. Nurses had already arrived and were trying to revive him. They took him to the Dispensary and Physician Assistant Robert Barnard tried to save him, but could not. I had never seen a person die so violently, and I was physically sick after it happened. Security felt that this inmate had snitched on another inmate for making a ladder to go over the wall. An investigation proved the wrong inmate had been killed. Officer Wallace found the ladder in the tall grass behind the gym and the knife inside a trash can. This also disclosed the guilty murderer. An inmate cannot snitch in a prison! It got "hot" for the inmate who had told me about this, and they immediately had to transfer him to another facility.

Another inmate named Ancil Hall was killed on the yard because he owed four dollars. Another inmate named Howard Lowery owed some money, and one inmate knocked him down while another inmate cut his throat almost decapitating him.

One night during gym hours, a trusted inmate told me that another inmate had stolen my gloves from my coat. I confronted the inmate, and naturally he wanted the name of the snitch. I could not tell him the truth. I had to protect the snitch from being killed. There are many "gray areas" in a prison to protect some inmates.

We had many inmates who were killed for gambling debts. One inmate, who was on our gym crew, was running a "store" out of his cell. A store allowed inmates to buy items from the canteen from other inmates for a profit. Of course, many times inmates felt cheated. The inmate running the store was killed in his cell.

Prison also is a dangerous place for inmates who had previously served in law enforcement in some capacity. These inmates usually had to go on protective custody, or they would be killed. When I first came to work at OSR and all of the inmates lived in the old cell house, protection inmates were called PRO's which meant PERMANENT RACK ON'S. They stayed in their cells all of the time and their food was brought to their cells. However, some proved trustworthy and would be allowed privileges on the yard. I knew an ex-highway patrolman who interacted with others appropriately on the yard. We were playing softball once on a slippery field and the same ex-highway patrolmen fell and got abrasions on his leg. For some reason he got angry at me but later apologized.

Many protection inmates have been killed when placed with general population, including a minister who was convicted of molesting children. In the 1973 riot at the Oklahoma State Penitentiary, an inmate who later came to OSR, told me about the inmates who were killed at that riot. At the Penitentiary of New Mexico in 1980, which happened to be the worst riot in U.S. history, many inmates were killed by their fellow inmates. After that riot, many inmates were transferred to OSR.

Most killings in a prison are done with a "shank," prison jargon for a knife. Shanks are made of just about anything: toothbrushes, silverware, old steel springs, steel rods, steak or pork chop bones, wooden shingles, combs, etc. Many inmates bury their shanks outside their unit for their own protection. Some inmates are choked or beaten to death. A few hang themselves or die from illegal drugs. There was an inmate, Peanut, who was on protection because he quoted other inmates in a book written by someone else. If he had gone on general population, he would have been dead in five minutes. Everyone wanted to kill Peanut. Prison can definitely be a dangerous place!

Chapter 14
ANY EMPLOYEE CAN GET KILLED

Just as any inmate could be killed, employees were aware they too might be killed. I've been told that in the history of the gym there was at least one employee killed there. I was told also that many years ago a coach was killed on the baseball field. We had at least one employee killed by a shank when I worked at OSR. It was next to impossible for an inmate to smuggle a gun into prison. As long as I worked there, I did not know of any time when a gun was found. An employee always had to be "watching his back," so to speak. Sometimes I could just "feel" something was wrong. If so, I would call security, and Officers would respond. The way inmates grouped together sometimes was an indication of trouble.

Allen Gamble, a Correctional Officer, was killed in D Unit as he tried to break up a shank fight between two inmates. He was stabbed and taken to a hospital in Altus, Oklahoma, where he died that night. They had his funeral at the Granite gym because it was bigger to accommodate more people. It was tragic because he left behind a wife and children. He was well liked, an excellent Correctional Officer, and was truly missed. Officer Calloway was badly cut during a fight and never returned to work at OSR. I never blamed him!

A student inmate had a vendetta against a female teacher. He put a knife to her throat and pushed her into a bathroom. Another inmate and a male school teacher took the knife away from him. The male teacher was cut, required stitches on his face, and still has a scar. He could have easily been killed. Inmates were not supposed to assist employees in a situation like this. Because the inmate did assist, he was discharged from prison and allowed to go home. If he had remained in prison, he would have been placed on protective custody.

At the 1973 riot, many well-liked employees were not killed because they were hidden in cells by sympathetic inmates. At the prison riot in New Mexico in 1980, many employees were killed. Prison can be a dangerous place for employees, as well as inmates!

Chapter 15
AN ESCAPE OR A KILLING?

The mission in Oklahoma prisons while I worked for DOC was three-fold: 1. Protect the Public 2. Protect the Employee 3. Protect the Offender. To protect the public, inmates must be securely confined to avoid escape and harm to society. Tax dollars are spent on prisons to keep inmates away from them. It is dangerous when an offender escapes and the mission of Protecting the Public is not met. Most people think that an escape is worse than an inmate being killed because an escape is betraying the public trust. Therefore, no one wants an escape, and most everyone really does not want an inmate killed. However, some people think that a financial burden has been lifted when an inmate is killed. When an inmate escapes, there is a possibility he can murder someone. Therefore, an inmate escaping or an inmate being killed is a very sensitive subject when the two sides are compared.

While on the ball field in 1984, which was the year that I started working at OSR, an inmate by the name of Floyd Gene Hughes hid in a dug out when we were bringing the inmates inside the walls. We counted fifty-three inmates when it was actually fifty-two. He had waited until dark and climbed over the fence. He was later caught in the town of Granite, and no one was hurt. I had to take a leave of absence without pay for a week for that escape. The following year, while on the ball field, two inmates had obtained wire cutters, cut through a chain link fence, and escaped while we were not looking. They had a car waiting for them at the

Trustee Building and were caught. Their relatives, driving the car, were charged with Attempting to Help an Inmate Escape from a Penal Institution. No one was injured. I had to take a leave of absence without pay for a week for that escape also. There have been cases of inmates hiding in trash cans from the kitchen and transferring to the trash truck. However, they were discovered and unable to escape.

When an inmate is killed, the prison doctor or the Physicians' Assistant must sign the death warrant and the deceased inmate's family must be notified. This is a grueling task. The Oklahoma Bureau of Investigation must also be notified immediately. These Bureau agents are on call 24 hours a day. I am sure they are not happy about mid-morning calls. When an inmate named Gene Marriot was stabbed to death one night, I had to call an OSBI agent at 4:00 A.M. I was not too happy about that either.

I have had experiences of inmates escaping and inmates being killed in prison. Society must decide (or the debate will continue) which is the worse scenario.

The mission of DOC

Chapter 16
THE STORY OF KILLER

The recreation staff usually had several inmates on our gym crew who would help us clean the gym and also help us with our recreational activities. We once needed one more inmate to complete our gym crew, so we hired an inmate who everyone called "Killer." He was a pot-bellied, heavy-set, congenial old man in his sixties. None of the inmates knew or called him by his real name. They just called him Killer. Everyone in the entire prison system in Oklahoma knew him because he had been in prison most of his adult life. He always had his own chair in our office. Everyone on the gym crew honored that. Inmates did not take advantage of him partly because of his age. A lot of inmates were afraid of him simply because of what his name implied. He got along well with other inmates and staff. Actually, I think that he had a better relationship with my co-workers than I did; however, I think that he liked me. My boss would always say to him in an affectionate way "Killer no." Killer said that he wanted to get out of prison and settle down. My boss told him that, because he had been in prison all of his life, he was already settled down. He said that the only way he could be more settled was to be in a coma.

He was a good cleaner in the gym and wasn't afraid of hard work. On one occasion, a work crew was running cement at one of the units. Being in his prison boots didn't prevent him from jumping right in the cement to help them. He laughed a lot and had a good sense of humor, but there always seemed something hidden behind his smile and laughter. On the surface, he didn't seem to be a killer. However, convicted felons are deceitful! He always had an "air" about him that made me uneasy. Legend had it that Killer had killed over one hundred people; hence the name *killer*. I used to walk with him in the gym. He would never tell me a definite number of people he had killed because that was his secret. He did say that most of his killings occurred in California during bank robberies. Because California was so large and overpopulated, he could fade into the state undetected. He said that when he committed the bank robberies, he was never nervous and would be so nonchalant that he could shoot a gun with one hand and eat a hamburger with the other. He said that he had been incarcerated only once in California on an unrelated crime. Because he had never been charged or convicted on his bank robberies, he did not have a long sentence for this crime. He was serving two eleven year sentences in Oklahoma, fifteen life sentences in Kansas for shooting a policeman, and a fifty year sentence in Illinois. He escaped in Illinois. While he was changing the license tag of his car, a policeman shot him three times with a .357 magnum. While they were waiting for an ambulance to take him to the hospital, he asked the policeman to buy him a hamburger. He said that he got a sadistic joy out of killing and didn't know why. I often wondered if his issues stemmed from incidents that happened in his childhood. His situation reminded me of the Oklahoma-based movie *The Killer Inside Me* with the actor Casey Affleck. (By the way, I was filmed in that movie. I was seen driving my green 1953 Ford ten times.)

Killer never married and never had any children of his own. He always said that he wanted to get married someday and live in a big house in the country. Shortly after he had done time at OSR, he developed cancer and was transferred to another facility that had a cancer unit. We hated to see him go because we had grown fond of him. We later received word that he had died there. How sad because he never did get married and never got to live in a big house in the country. We miss Killer. I'm sure that there will never be anyone else like him! (The Recreation staff had a photograph of Killer, but we were unable to find it. I'm sure it would have been interesting to the reader what he looked like. However, maybe it's better to let the reader use imagination.)

My 53 Ford was in the movie *The Killer Inside Me*. Deputy Sheriff Lou Ford, played by actor Casey Affleck, had the same childhood issues as killer.

Chapter 17
FROM JUVENILE DELINQUENCY AND FROM MILITARY TO CRIMINAL

I worked six months as a Recreation Supervisor at the Oklahoma Children's Center, a juvenile facility at Taft, Oklahoma, seven miles west of Muskogee, Oklahoma. Later I coordinated juvenile recreation for the Oklahoma Department of Human Services in Muskogee County for one year. Activities at Taft were in the gym. Activities at Muskogee County were held in gyms in Boyonton, Oklahoma, and Porum, Oklahoma. Later, I worked for Court-related and Community Services, which was a division under the Department of Human Services. For four and a half years, I coordinated recreation for juveniles for a nine-county area in Southwest Oklahoma. The recreation activities in this 9-county area were done in these different counties. Some of these recreational activities were float trips down the Illinois River or Lake Tenkiller Recreation Camp. Other activities included rock concerts, baseball games, circuses, museums, and the zoo. The Coca-Cola Company in Altus provided us free drinks for the summer. The purpose of all these activities was to deter the juveniles from becoming adult criminals. I enjoyed providing recreation for juveniles under the age of 18. Even though we tried to curb juveniles' criminal behavior, we were not always successful. Many juvenile delinquents were later incarcerated in prison as adults. I viewed this as a failure. However, I realized that no amount of effort on my part could rehabilitate some juvenile delinquents; some would eventually live an adult criminal life. On the other hand, some did live productive adult lives. I learned that adult inmates that had been juvenile delinquents gave the most problems. One inmate that I worked with as a juvenile and had taken to many recreational events gave me the hardest time of all.

Many of our inmates in prison were previously enlisted in various branches of the military. Most of them claimed that their military experiences, especially during stressful times of the Vietnam War, caused them to commit crimes that sent them to prison. Most of them claimed that active military duty affected them psychologically. They had killed the enemy and seen their military buddies killed. Many ex-military inmates suffered from post-traumatic stress disorder. Our Korean War veterans did not suffer from this disorder as much since it was before Vietnam. Because of this, veterans suffered from alcohol, drug, and domestic abuse issues. Many of them suffered from anxiety and personality disorders. They felt that they were betrayed by their country. About 1,500 or 10 percent of the population of Oklahoma prisons were ex-military. Many of them were still fighting the war within themselves. OSR originally was built as a Reformatory for boys but was later changed to an adult prison. During World War II, inmates trained on the yard using wooden rifles. Evidently they wished that they had been a part of that conflict.

Of all of the inmates who helped us referee and umpire sports, ex-military inmates were the best. Their military training helped them exert their authority; that kind of expertise was needed for referees and umpires to be successful. They also were the most dependable of the inmates because of the discipline that they had received in the armed forces.

Ex-military men also made excellent Officers and employees because of their training in the military. We had one man named Chuck Baker who was a Lt. Colonel in the Marines. He was promoted to Captain at OSR quickly because he knew how to deal with employees and inmates. Some military employees were not as popular. There was an ex-Army employee who was despised by the inmates. They said if there was a riot, he would be the first to be taken hostage.

All in all, I found that adult criminals were easier to reason with than juvenile delinquents because they were more mature.

MICHAEL A. NORCROSS

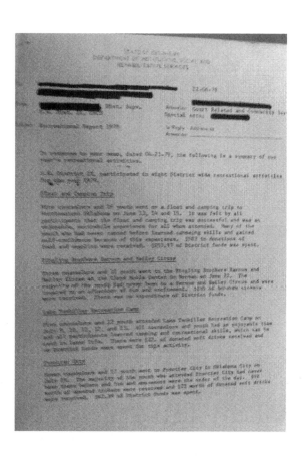

Recreational Report 1979
Page 2

Baseball Game

Five counselors and 13 youth attended an exhibition baseball game between the OKC 89'ers and the Philadelphia Phillies at All Sports Stadium in Oklahoma City on the evening of August 16. This was probably the first time most of the youth and counselors had ever seen a major league team play. Most everyone enjoyed the game and learned something about the game of baseball. $40 of donated soft drinks were received. $85.16 of District funds were spent.

Springlake Fun Park

Three counselors and 17 youth went to Springlake Fun Park in Oklahoma City on September 15. A more beautiful day could not have been asked for and youth and counselors alike enjoyed exciting rides, shows and games and had a fun-filled afternoon. $40 of donated soft drinks were received. $105.85 of District funds were spent.

Lincoln Park Zoo

Five counselors and 20 youth went to Lincoln Park Zoo in Oklahoma City on October 19th. Probably the most beneficial purpose of the trip to the zoo was the cultural and educational experience shared by the youth who attended. $36 in donated soft drinks were received and $33.43 of District funds were spent.

Styx Concert

Five counselors and 20 youth attended a rock concert featuring the Chicago rock group Styx at the Lloyd Noble Center in Norman on the evening of Friday, November 30. Styx provided an electrifying performance of music to a packed house of responsive rock fans. Counselors and youth felt the group performed to their expectations and had an enjoyable evening of rock music. $24 in donated soft drinks were received and $156.25 of District funds were spent.

We anticipate the remainder of our funds, $108.65, to be used in individual county activities for the month of December.

Besides our district-wide activities, Jackson County had a very good individual county recreation program. A total of 22 counselors and 97 youth attended their activities which included swimming parties, skating parties, a tour of McDonalds, picnics, nature tours, movies and a tour of the C-5 Galaxy at Altus Air Force Base. Jackson County received $138 of donated soft drinks for their individual county's activities.

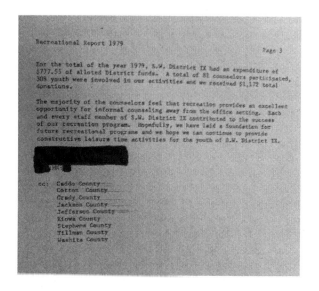

These are the juvenile activities that we did while I worked for CR&CS. We did all of this to try to get juveniles turned around before they became adult criminals. I did all of the recreational work on these. My District Supervisor took all of the credit for it, so I have blacked out his name.

Inmates training on the yard using wooden rifles during World War II just in case they needed to be called up and released from prison.

Chapter 18
"I'LL BE BACK"-HIGH RECIDIVISM RATE

In the 1990's, the recidivism rate in Oklahoma prisons was about 86%. In other words, out of one hundred inmates who were released from prison, eighty-six would return to prison at some point in their lives. This was a high rate. Many inmates are more comfortable in prison than on the street. In prison, inmates receive three "hots" (meals) and a "cot" (a bed.) They have an air-conditioned cell, usually a job, and all of the recreation that they want— at no cost to them. In a depressed economy, a released inmate must have a paying job to afford a house or rent an apartment, pay bills, and pay other expenses. However, an incarcerated inmate receives this free. The only discomfort is being confined. This probably explains a high recidivism rate among inmates. I remember a recently returned inmate in the gym who said, "I'm so glad to be back in. I'm going to dance." He then proceeded to do a little dance.

Many inmates intentionally commit crimes to return to prison. Some inmates on minimum security, who are not confined by walls, escape by simply walking away before they are to be discharged. They are charged with escape and remain in prison. Some inmates stay in prison to continue to play softball or basketball. I remember reading a story of such an inmate when I was a child. He robbed a jewelry store so that he could be convicted and sent back to prison to continue playing on the baseball team. Some inmates only have $50 (given by the state) when they are released from prison. Without the prospects of employment, many will return because of financial hardship.

In the 1920's and 1930's, "fresh fish" (new inmates) were harshly disciplined from officers. They were questioned about their sentence, then slapped and humiliated. Slapping all inmates was not uncommon. Probably because of that, the recidivism rate was lower. Pro-inmate organizations disallow that treatment today. It is considered demeaning and demoralizing. Some are even considering changing the title *inmate* to *client.*

A high recidivism rate indicates something is wrong with the system. Even many employees feel that inmates have better conditions than employees in a prison. They the only difference is that employees get to go home at night.

Chapter 19
TEACHERS BRING THEIR STUDENTS TO PRISON FOR AN EDUCATION

We had a program at OSR that allowed public school teachers to bring their students into the prison. Inmates would talk to the students about prison life. This program was capably run by an inmate named Tommy Cartwright. This program was not mandatory but was open to caring inmates who wanted to prevent students from following in their footsteps. The role play that the inmates performed was held in the gym. I usually observed many of these.

Some inmates would role play illegally driving a car with passengers who had a marijuana cigarette or some other drug, and the driver was unaware. They pretended that they were arrested and everyone, including the driver, went to jail, were convicted, and sent to prison.

One of the teachers who brought her students told the inmates that she was having trouble with a particular student. She felt he was wayward and might possibly be headed to juvenile hall. The inmates stressed to students that prison life was intolerable. This student was smug, smart-aleck, and was essentially making fun of the program. The inmates screamed, "Do you think all of this is funny?" They screamed expletives in his face. Eventually, the student started crying. In essence, this may have been the deterrent for the wayward student. Later, we found out that the student was never again a discipline problem. The inmates felt that this program deterred some kids from prison.

Tommy Cartwright was the perfect mentor for this program. When he was released from prison, he never returned.

My wife, who was a school teacher at Lone Wolf School, brought her class to participate in the program. While there, the students were shown where the inmates got their supplies from the canteen. It was just a hole in the wall. They were also shown the old cell houses, built in 1909, and since have been abandoned. The students were astounded that someone could live in these cells. They all said that they never wanted to be incarcerated. When they returned to school, they told their fellow students about the experience. Because of this "education," hopefully none of them will be sentenced to prison.

Chapter 20
LAWSUITS GALORE – SUED FOR THREE CANS OF POP

Inmate law clerks that helped other inmates sue the state or a state employee are known as "jail house lawyers." Inmates can sue for any reason, especially if they think money is involved or their sentence might be reduced. The wardens probably get sued more than other employees. Some of these suits are filed in State and Federal court in intelligent, legal language, but most are considered frivolous.

Every year we had an event called "The Prisoners Run against Child Abuse." For this event, inmates ran on the yard. The recreation staff tallied the laps that were run. The inmates who ran the most laps got trophies for first, second, and third place. They also won soft drinks or pop. The event was a public relations event as the proceeds and donations were sent to agencies that fought child abuse. All of the participants also received T-shirts which said "Prisoners Run against Child Abuse." The winners in general population and protective custody won twelve cans of pop for first place, nine cans of pop for second place, and six cans of pop for third place. (After the last run, we only had fifty T-shirts for the inmates, and there were hundreds running! Imagine how upset the ones were that were not awarded T-shirts.)

My co-workers and I conducted the run with protective custody in B-Unit, which was held in a separate location from general population. When we finished the race, we distributed the pops and trophies to all of the winners. We thought we were finished. No way! About two weeks later, I had a Federal law suit on my desk from an inmate who had participated in the run. He claimed that I had rewound my watch (which I didn't) and that caused him to receive second place instead of first place. In other words, he had been awarded nine cans of pop, instead of twelve cans: a difference of THREE cans. He hired an expensive, renowned lawyer from New York and sued me (for three cans of pop.) I had to submit my written version of the incident and send it to a Federal Judge. Just consider the expense of a lawyer versus three cans of soda??? HOW ASININE!! For my own protection, I spoke to a lawyer about it. He thought that it was frivolous. I later found out that if an employee was sued by an inmate, the suit would be submitted to the warden's office. It was eventually thrown out of court for being frivolous. I later learned that twenty other employees from OSR were being sued in the lawsuit, including the warden. This inmate was not in prison for skipping Sunday School Services. He was convicted of choking his wife to death in a shelter for battered women. Imagine my reaction when I went to work one unsuspecting morning and found a Federal Lawsuit on my desk! (I had a copy of the lawsuit against me, but I misplaced it. It might have been interesting to the reader if I could have put it after this chapter. However, if I placed it here, I would have needed to black out names and numbers. I might possibly have been sued again. Ha!)

This is the front of the Prisoners' Run Against Child Abuse shirt in 1992 (8 years after I came to work at OSR).

MICHAEL A. NORCROSS

Chapter 21
HUMOR IS GOOD MEDICINE

Proverbs 17:22 in the Bible says, "A merry heart does good like medicine, but a broken spirit dries up the bones." This saying is most relevant in prison as anyone can imagine the stress that employees endure. Inmates and employees learn to provide humor to relieve stress.

Some inmates felt the recreation we provided was lacking because of tight security. We all had to carry multiple keys to lock every door in the gym. One of the funniest sayings that I ever heard came from an inmate on our gym crew named "Towhead." He told me, "Any chimpanzee could carry your keys and do your job for just a banana a day." I later found a plaque that had a picture of a chimpanzee on it, had the slogan inscribed on the bottom of it, and gave it to him. He found it extremely facetious.

I tried to maintain some lightheartedness in my job; therefore, I kept a board that had a mouse trap on it with a red button that said, "Got a complaint – Press red button." (Of course the trap was welded and couldn't snap.) Whenever someone had a complaint, I would show the board to them. I also tried to stay lighthearted in my approach with the inmates. One night I was admitting about twenty inmates into the gym. Towhead was among them. My introduction proceeded as follows: "Welcome to the OSR gym. Tonight we have many constructive recreational activities planned for you. I hope that your stay with us will be an enjoyable one." They all found my irony quite comical.

Dannie Blevins, one of my co-workers, was a comedian. He found humor many times at my own expense. He often compared me to a sloth. One night we had protective custody inmates in the gym. One of the inmates had been convicted of having had sex with a dead person in a funeral home. Dannie told me, "Norcross!!!!! Hurry!!! Move your arms and legs. Don't let him think you're dead!"

One day we had a deaf mute inmate in our office. I was not aware that a deaf mute person could not hear. I was trying to talk to him. He acted like he was not hearing me. I'm sure he was frightened. The closer I got to him the more I yelled. He and my co-workers got another laugh at my expense.

One day I went to the bathroom and the toilet paper accidentally got stuck in the back of my pants. As I walked, the toilet paper kept coming from the bathroom roll. By the time I reached my office, I had about thirty feet of toilet paper trailing behind me. Needless to say, our gym crew found that quite humorous.

When I first started working at OSR, I lacked confidence. Inmates were aware of this because they were "experts" on one's weaknesses. One inmate named Jack Taylor said, "If you will run this paper off on a copy machine, I'll pump your balls up with an air compressor." Jack once slipped on a wet spot on the floor in the rotunda. He said if he would have gotten hurt, he would have sued the state for millions of dollars. Quite interestingly, after Jack was discharged from prison, a Correctional Officer saw him in a restaurant in Oklahoma City with two women. We always knew him to be the "playboy" type.

A "Slow Play" is a term the inmates use when they are trying to get something from another inmate by means of procrastination.

My nervousness when I first started working was also obvious. An inmate told me, "You need a thorazine! You've got a slight nervous problem!" My CO-WORKERS even made me a certificate for a one time visit to Dr. Kevorkian and gave it to my wife.

Officer Dave Morris was manning the front door one morning and the acting prison doctor came through. Dave said this doctor was always in a "fizz." As a practical joke, Dave decided that he would "shake him down" (body search). The doctor became so angry that he complained to the Warden. When the doctor came out of the Warden's office, he shook him down again.

We used to have cattle in pens outside the walls in the sight of Tower 4. There was a big bull in a small pen. An Officer became trapped in the pen, and the bull almost killed him. The Tower 4 Officer's version was humorous. He said there was so much chaos in the pen that he didn't know whether to shoot the Officer or the bull. As it turned out, the Officer was fine and continued to work at OSR for over thirty years.

An inmate escaped one time in a facility car. As soon as the escape was discovered, Officers and institution dogs were sent in hot pursuit. The escapee was found at a woman's house treed by her own dogs.

Joe Harp was the Warden at OSR from 1949 to 1969. Charles Dawson had worked under Joe Harp. Charles said the inmates respected Warden Harp and believed what he said. Warden Harp would often broadcast on the yard through the intercom system. If he said, "You m--- f---ers clear the yard, or we're going to start shooting," the yard WAS cleared. A Tower Officer with a rifle always took the Warden at his word. If he said, "Shoot!" shots rang everywhere.

Deputy Warden Raines, who worked at OSR about 70 years ago, was not as credible. It was said he was quite a drinker. So much so that he invited a trustee named Mayberry to come to his house to drink. They drank until they were quite inebriated. The inmate somehow became angered at the Deputy's dog and started kicking it. The Deputy became quite inhospitable and literally kicked the inmate out of his house.

Terry Whitecotton, an inmate on our gym crew, knew how to peel an orange in a certain way that would leave the orange intact on the outside. Terry managed to confiscate my co-worker's lunch, made a slit in the orange, and put shreds of paper in it. When Dannie peeled the orange to eat it, there was nothing but paper left on the inside. The pulp had been completely removed.

One of our inmates at the Trustee Building was totally blind. He had been convicted and sent to prison for Driving Under the Influence!!!! (Now, how does that happen?) One of our inmates Terry Long was such a bad basketball player that we called him "The Ray Charles of Basketball." We even nicknamed an inmate from Oklahoma City Jethro of *The Beverly Hillbillies* simply because he resembled him. He was good natured and everyone liked him.

When the inmates lived in the old cell houses, sometimes they would not get showers after softball games. One night, after a game, a group of inmates needed showers. An inmate named Buddy Womack wanted me to persuade the Captain to let them shower. He told me, "Mike! Don't go in there like you're sick, but go in there with a bucket full of balls and ten pounds of hair on your ass!" I guess I didn't have either because they didn't get their showers.

We had a mentally challenged inmate at OSR who watched *The Flintstones* all day. He later was discharged and moved to Kansas City. About a year after his discharge, my family and I got a special deal to fly to Kansas City and back in one day. When we were boarding the plane to return to Oklahoma, I noticed that the pilot of the plane was an exact replica of our "challenged" inmate. It scared me to death!

After my surgery in 2007, I remained unconscious for thirty days and was hospitalized for seven weeks. I was on a respirator, a ventilator, and was hydrated intravenously. Dannie Blevins and his wife Judy came to the hospital to visit me. This allowed my wife Nelda to go to her brother's house and shower. Dannie later told me that while she was gone, he started to pull the plug. I'm glad he didn't! I hope my wife is too!!

The most infamous homosexual at OSR was named Cinnamon. Everyone wanted to "cell" with Cinnamon.

The oddest inmate was Jeannie. He (or she) had a sex change operation on the street but was unable to have the process completed. This meant some body parts were male and other parts were female. Homosexuals are accepted more in prison than on the street. Jeannie killed HIS wife (female partner) because they BOTH agreed to have a sex change. He started; she didn't and laughed at "him." He killed her and hence ended up in prison. We also had a homosexual basketball player that carried a purse and wore mascara and lipstick.

In order to rob an area bank, one of our inmates kidnapped the bank president, made him open the bank, and robbed it. He then took the president back to his home, tied/gagged him, locked him a closet, and set fire to his house. This inmate told me that was just a real dumb thing to do. In fact, he was so dumb he couldn't learn his route as an elevator operator in a two-story building. Naturally, he was fired. (This was his first post-high school job.)

At OSR, Many inmates took "Talk Back TV" college courses from Western Oklahoma State College in Altus, Oklahoma. Four inmates that graduated with Associate Degrees were taken for the graduation ceremony in a prison van. One of the inmates was Chuck Tashawn, a Comanche Indian. When Chuck walked across the stage, his mother yelled from the audience, "Comanche!" The audience found it quite humorous.

There was inmate from Texas who was convicted of murder in Oklahoma. He tried to rob a psychiatrist's house in Wichita Falls, Texas. He said the psychiatrist was so "paranoid" that his house was going to be robbed that all his windows were only 6" by 6". Isn't it ironic that a psychiatrist would be paranoid?

RECREATION FROM BEHIND PRISON WALLS

Before they banned smoking in the prison, we had butt cans next to the walls in the gym. These were gallon food containers from the kitchen. Sometimes after the general population would leave for the night, the gym crew would clean. Before they cleaned, they would get basketballs and roll them toward the cans and pretend that they were bowling. The cans full of cigarette butts would make a mess when overturned by the basketballs. One inmate said that he thought this practice would eventually get him into the Bowling Hall of Fame. (He wasn't kidding-he really believed that!)

If inmates are desperate for drugs, they smuggle in desperate ways. For example, a female visitor would casually come into the Visitor Room, visit with an inmate friend, then transfer a balloon with marijuana or some other drug by kissing her "friend." The inmate would then swallow the balloon. Later, nature would take its course, and the balloon with drugs would pass in the toilet in the inmate's cell. The inmate would then have successfully smuggled his drugs.

We had an Officer named Hank Snow who came into the gym with a large pair of bolt cutters to cut off a lock on the door. When he walked in, he asked if anyone was ready for a vasectomy. The inmates said they were not because when they got out of prison they wanted to get married and have children.

Employees sarcastically called all inmates "peckerwoods." Even inmates thought that was funny.

These short quips from my years at OSR are fond memories because we always managed to find humor in ourselves and others. They reduced stress in a very serious surrounding.

Whenever inmates misbehaved, Warden Clara Waters made them dress as girls as punishment.

An inmate said this about the recreation staff so I made this plaque and gave it to him

Whenever an inmate would come to me with a complaint, I would have him press the red button

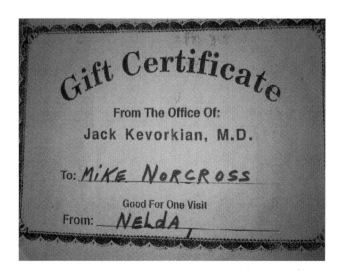

A certificate given to my wife by my co-workers for a one time visit for me to a suicide Dr. Kevorkian as a joke. I am glad I did not keep the appointment!

DVD of the *Beverly Hillbillies.* We had an inmate that looked and acted like Jethro, the character at the bottom of the DVD. He was called Jethro by everyone.

Chapter 22
GETTING PUNCHED IN THE NOSE! "OUCH!"
BOY, DID I BLEED.

I can honestly say that in the twenty-three years that I worked in the penal system at OSR, I was only punched one time. That's just a pretty good record. However, this one time was a shocker for me.

Various clubs at OSR liked to prepare banquets as one of their social gatherings. We tried to accommodate them as much as we could. One day, the Indian Club was sponsoring a banquet in the gym. No one was in attendance except their members. An uninvited inmate came to the door and told me that he wanted to join the banquet. I politely told him that he was not allowed at this event because he was not a member of the club. Just as I was closing the door, he hauled off and hit me in the nose with his fist! Blood spurted everywhere. I didn't appreciate that the inmate gym crew found it funny. I thought they were fond of me, but one can never totally trust inmates. Well, the inmate who clubbed me ran off. I reported it to security as quickly as possible. Two officers escorted me to the Dispensary where they stopped the bleeding. I got the rest of the day off.

Security dispatched officers to the scene and tackled the offending inmate. He was then taken to "lock-up." I later learned that he had not been taking his psychotropic medication. I was told he had even thrown his television out of his cell into the day room because it had "evil spirits." He later had a legal hearing and was sent to the Oklahoma State Penitentiary.

Like I said, one fist in the face in twenty-three years is a good record.

Chapter 23
THE LIFERS CLUB – THE MOST PROGRESSIVE CLUB

Oklahoma State Reformatory had many inmate clubs governed by a constitution and by-laws and employees for sponsors. These clubs allowed certain groups to bond. Some of the clubs were the Hispanic Club, Indian Club, Chess Club, Weightlifting Club, Arts and Crafts Club, Lifers Club, etc.

I was a sponsor of the Hispanic Club and Sandy Baldonado was the president. The members held these clubs in high esteem and allowed no disrespect to the sponsors, as sponsors were difficult to find and keep. I tried to initiate an Arts and Crafts Club at the Trustee Building, but an inmate got upset with me because he thought I didn't do enough to start one. There were hard feeling between us, and we never did get the club started.

The Indian club met behind the gym and built a Sweat Lodge for their 30 minute-religious-cleansing ceremony. The heat was generated by logs that had been fired and placed in the tent. We had to be cautious to make sure no one asphyxiated or dehydrated. The logs actually had to start burning several hours before they actually started "sweating." Oklahoma has a large Indian population that holds this ceremony sacred. We were fortunate to offer this experience at OSR.

Probably the club that provided the most benefits was the Lifers Club. An inmate had to be sentenced to life in order to be a member of this club. This club was probably the most popular and progressive with inmates and employees. The President of the Lifers Club was Willie "Head" Austin who was well-respected and liked by the inmates on the yard. Many people said that he somewhat ran the yard with the inmates. The Lifers Club had their own room at the bottom of the school. They started a program to encourage members to speak publicly of their offenses if ever paroled. The Lifers Club sponsored some of the pool tournaments that we had in the gym. "Head" managed to have a pool table donated from a pool table company and put in their club room. The pool tournaments that they sponsored were an example of how they made the most of their time in prison in a creative, constructive way. The Lifers Club even had T-shirts printed which had their name and emblem on the back of the shirt. After "Head" was paroled, the club did not function quite as well.

    A group of inmates wanted to start a Gay Club and had a certain staff member in mind to become the sponsor. A co-worker of mine said, "Birds of a feather flock together."

    All in all, clubs performed an important function for inmates at OSR and they gave them a sense of belonging. Even though they were called clubs, a lot of employees thought that these clubs were just gangs, but I did not agree with that philosophy.

Suggested Constitution and By-Laws
for the
Arts & Crafts Club
of the Trusty Building of the Oklahoma State Reformatory at Granite
Oklahoma

Articles of the Constitution

Article 1- Name

This organization shall be known as the Universal Arts & Crafts Club of the Trusty Building of the Oklahoma State Reformatory.

Article 2- Purpose

To awaken and promote an interest in Arts & Crafts and fellowship of interested inmates at OSR-TB.

Article 3- Membership

All inmates at the Oklahoma State Reformatory Trusty Building shall be eligible for membership. Also, there will be equal rights for members for approved projects of the club.

Article 4- Officers

There shall be a President, Vice President, Secretary, Treasurer, and Sergeant at Arms, to be elected in manner/as provided. The club adviser shall be the Recreation Supervisor of the Recreation Staff. The adviser shall be an overseer of the club and financial staff.

Article 5- Amendments

This Constitution may be amended by a two-thirds vote of the membership. All amendments are to be submitted in writing and signed by three members and to be read at a regular meeting.

By-Laws

Article 1- Officers

Section 1. All officers shall be elected annually by a majority of the members on a ballot.

Section 2. Election of officers are to be held in the month of September.

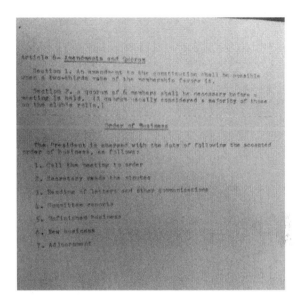

Constitution and by-laws required for every club that was started. This happened to be for the arts and crafts club which unfortunately never got started.

This is the emblem on the back of the Lifer's Club shirt.

Chapter 24
CHEATING ON RECREATIONAL EVENTS

The recreational unit provided inmates the opportunities for about any kind of tournament (pool, ping pong, chess, horseshoes, weightlifting, etc.) with soft drinks from the canteen as prizes. Inmates were glad to be able to play in the tournaments. It made our gym crew and the inmates who assisted with the tournaments feel important. On many occasions these tournaments ran smoothly without cheating.

When I went to work at OSR, trophies were awarded for the winners, usually first, second, and third place. When David Miller became Warden, he wanted us to conduct more tournaments. We had them so frequently that soft drinks became the prizes. The winners usually received twelve cans for first place, nine cans for second place, and six cans for third place.

On the negative side, some inmates wanted soft drinks so badly that they would cheat any way possible to obtain them. Imagine inmates cheating!!! When we weren't able to finish a chess tournament in one sitting, I put the chess board with the pieces in place in a room to be continued at a later date. When I turned my back, the players moved the chess pieces to their advantage.

During pool tournaments, a player would wait until his opponent wasn't looking and move a pool ball to his advantage. During weightlifting tournaments, an assisting inmate would say that one of his buddies lifted a certain amount of weight when he had not. Inmate umpires in softball and inmate referees in basketball and volleyball intentionally made calls in favor of his favorite team. The inmates who kept score sometimes changed the scorebooks to the advantage of the team that he favored. Sometimes the cheating was discovered by the recreation staff, sometimes not.

In a ping pong tournament, it was very difficult to know if a ping pong ball hit the edge of the table. Only the referee nearest the table could know the difference to call the point. The inmate referee always called the point in favor of his own buddies.

In the Prisoners Run against Child Abuse, the inmates who would help us count the runners' rounds would add laps to their friends' advantage. The inmates who helped us distribute the T-shirts for the run gave shirts to their friends who didn't even run. In volleyball, if a player touched the top of the net it would be the other team's ball. Sometimes the referee said that a player touched the top of the net in order to give the serve to the other team. During softball games and tournaments, umpires called balls and strikes in favor of their buddies. During basketball games, referees called fouls on players who actually did not foul.

The cheating that affected me most personally was the BINGO competition that I initiated at the Trustee Building. I had obtained slide type BINGO cards and a turn hopper with wooden balls. (Many of the inmates wanted to be callers for the games and hard feelings ensued if they weren't chosen.) When the numbers were called, the called balls would be put on a board. On many occasions seventy-five inmates had cards at one time. From that point, the cheating began. Sometimes the caller would call numbers that actually did not come out of the hopper. When somebody BINGOED, I compared the card to the wooden balls on the board for a legitimate win. If the inmate won, he would wait until my back was turned and pass the winning card to other inmates. They would pass the same card back to me. Sometimes there were fifteen winners in one called game. I finally had to eliminate BINGO as a recreational activity at the Trustee Building. It just proved that inmates took advantage of me when I tried to make their prison time a little more tolerable. The criminal element that put them there continued to thrive.

> CHESS RULES
>
> s are taken from the Laws of Chess of the Wo
>
> cking a square crossed by an enemy pawn whi
> ares in one (1) move from its orginal squar
> as though the latter had been moved only on
> be made only on the move immediately follo
> ed capturing "en passant". This "en passan
> used at will.
>
> the last rank, a pawn must be immediately
> ve, for a queen, rook, bishop, or a knight
> t the players choice and without taking in
> ining on the board.
>
> completed--

Chess Rules

RECREATION FROM BEHIND PRISON WALLS

```
          OSP POOL TOURNAMENT
             HOUSE RULES

 eak of the balls will be established by flip of a coin.
 ls will be racked by unbiased overseer of game.
 on break of balls, the first ball to be pocketed by either
 ll establish that shooters group of balls to be shot (str
 n (stripes&solid) are pocketed upon break the shooter may
 ICE of balls to shoot at.
 ht(8) ball pocketed upon break results in win. (Unless ,
 keted simultaneously, it results in loss.
 oters must call the number of ball being shot and the po
 t at.
 binations must be called or will not be allowed.
 shot not called and pocketed will result in forfeit of
```

Pool Rules

Chapter 25
GAMES PLAYED BY CRIMINALS

By nature, criminals play games with employees, just as they were accustomed to on the streets. Sadly enough, some employees are duped enough by inmates to lose their jobs.

In our caustic room in the gym, one of my co-workers discovered enough ingredients in an empty milk sleeve to make home brew. He confronted an inmate on our gym crew, and he admitted his guilt. He apologized, said he shouldn't have done it, and promised it would never happen again. We had no choice but to "write him up." Because of his honesty, we let him remain on the gym crew. We thought that was the end of it. About a week later in another place in the same room, my co-worker discovered brew was being made again. The same inmate admitted guilt again. This time we had no choice but to write him up again and remove him from the gym crew. He continued to play the game criminals play to see if employees were alert.

When an inmate does any art or craft work for an employee, a form must be signed by the inmate and the employee determining the cost of the work. Money can't exchange hands, so the employee must give a money order for an inmates' draw from the canteen. I once had an inmate make me several jewelry boxes out of popsicle sticks to be gifts for Christmas. About a month before Christmas, we both agreed on a wage, signed the proper forms, and I paid the canteen. A few days before Christmas I inquired about the jewelry boxes, and he said that he hadn't even started on them. I had made the mistake of paying before receiving the finished goods. Only after the threat of a write-up did he finish the boxes before Christmas.

Soon after I became employed at OSR, I had to attend a training academy at Taft, Oklahoma. Part of the training instructed us on inmate manipulation, set-up, and games played on employees. We learned there were warning signals before a major disturbance: inmates group, tension increases, inmates become battle ready, and attitudes change. There are five different inmates on a set-up team: observer, contact, runner, turner, and point man. (Ironically, I worked with a very manipulative lady at the Department of Human Services who could play all five of these roles herself.)

Before our trainer started, the instructor informed us, "You can be set up!" I think everyone in the class took that lightly. Sometime later in the morning, a woman employee came into class and confronted the trainer about the pay roll. We were astounded that the instructor cursed and pushed her away. We all had to write incident reports on THIS incident. As it turned out, we were set up!

We also learned that inmates classify employees as soft, hard, and mellow. Soft employees are trusting. They are the easiest for a set up because they cannot say, "No." Hard employees have a gruff, tough exterior, but inmates feel they are covering up a weak interior. They are the second easiest to set up. Mellow employees know when to be hard and when to be soft. They are the hardest to

[margin note: This is the lady who worked with for CRFSS in Hobart ➜ I]

set up; therefore, inmates seldom try. I considered myself to be mellow.

An important part of an employee set up is duping the employee into becoming a "pack horse," someone who brings contraband into the prison. When the employee becomes a pack horse, the inmate has his "hook" in him. An inmate from California tried to get a hook in me, but was unable to do so. The employee must continue, or the inmate threatens to tell prison authorities.

The set up techniques are as follows: 1) the shopping list, 2) the lever, and 3) the sting. For a male employee, the shopping list demands smuggling drugs, alcohol, money, or weapons. For female employees, it is usually sex, then alcohol, money, or drugs. The lever is the pressure that an inmate demands of an employee to smuggle the contraband. The sting is the consequence for the employee determined by the inmate. The sting has caused some employees to resign, leave their jobs in disgrace, or for some: death. For the Correctional Employee who brought whiskey into his institution, the sting was termination of employment. For the Cook who refused to smuggle drugs, the sting was death by boiling in a 150 gallon steam vat. Luckily, he was rescued by co-workers. For a female employee who smuggled out letters, brought in contraband, yet refused demands for sex, the consequence was death.

A "Duck" is an employee that the inmate feels he can groom to do anything he insists. The inmate develops his duck patiently and carefully. For example, an inmate decided that he had been in prison long enough and told his duck to bring him a

Correctional Officer's uniform. The duck brought in a piece of the Officer's uniform every day that the inmate hid in his foot locker. When teams searched the inmate's cell, he knew how to manipulate them so that the uniform wasn't discovered. Somehow, the inmate put on the Officer's uniform, made it through two sally ports, and finally out the front gate. He slid under a barbed wire fence and into the safety of tall corn stalks. He stood by a car on the side of the road and convinced a passerby that he had run out of gas to get a ride to the next town. His escape was successful. About a year later, the same inmate was convicted of killing three people and was returned to prison. The scheme of the Officer's uniform was discovered, and the inmate testified against the correctional officer. He told how he had duped the "duck" and would scam more if given the chance. The duck was convicted and went to prison himself.

When I worked at OSR, we had one employee who was caught smuggling drugs. He was convicted and served one year in the county jail. We had one female employee who was caught having sex with an inmate. In Oklahoma it is a felony to have sexual relations with an inmate even if the sex is consensual. Many years ago, a tower officer was dropping down home brew to inmates in his bucket. There was also a lady officer who was caught dropping marijuana in her bucket. We had one employee who was a good correctional counselor, but was fired because he started going to inmates' cells and gambling. There are many other incidents like these that happen in Oklahoma. It is astounding that these employees were blind to the consequences of their actions!!

Part of our training class at Taft was to examine case studies of inmates who were experts at "setting up" employees, and employees who suffered the consequences of being scammed. The names in these cases were fictional.

Case History #1

Employee- 35 year old white male who worked in a women's prison in maintenance. His name was Bob.

Inmate- 23 year old white female who was sentenced to prison for murder. Her name was Mary. She was a drug addict and also a prostitute. She had been married three times, but there was no record that she had ever divorced. She was attractive.

Some male employees who work in a women's prison take pleasure in observing female inmates' movements and have sexual fantasies about the women prisoners. Women in prison like male attention because it is a diversion from their normal routine. Bob hired Mary to work in his unit, and she proved to be an excellent worker. She acted provocatively around him. She became intimate enough with him to tell him her personal problems with other female inmates. At some point, she even made sexual advances toward Bob. This led to sexual encounters in the storage room. Mary deceived Bob and told him she was pregnant with his child. At this point, Mary had set her hook and began making demands of Bob. Her first demand was four pounds of marijuana. If he didn't supply, she was going straight to the prison authorities.

Bob pled with Mary over her demands, but Mary stood her ground about telling authorities. He told her he had a good reputation to uphold and a wife and two children. She gave him the address of the pot supplier. Mary told Bob that they would continue using the store room for their own pleasure. After several months, it was obvious that Mary was pregnant. When she was questioned, she named Bob as the father. Bob could have denied the charge, but he was tired of lying to his wife about the money that he was spending for pot, tired of being around criminals, tired of the constant guilt inside of him, and tired of the worry and fear of being caught. Especially, he was tired of Mary, so he confessed.

Case History #2

Employee- 26 year old divorcee, mother of three. She was compassionate, trusting, and religious. She was tall, slim, and attractive. Her name was Carol.

Inmate-Charles was a 23 year old white male in prison for murder. He was intelligent, cunning, and was a manipulator. He was married to a prostitute, had no children, and furthermore loathed children.

Carol was assigned as a secretary in the prison vocational shop and asked Charles to work for her as she had observed his excellent work habits. She started talking to him about God since she was a "born-again" Christian. Charles told Carol that he had turned to crime because his wife had expensive tastes that he couldn't afford. To support three children and his wife, he began stealing; therefore, his wife divorced him. Carol was an emotional person and told him that she felt sorry for him.

Their similarities developed into intimacy. When Charles returned to work after a three weeks' absence, he complained to Carol that his youngest daughter had been very ill. She became a kind of a spiritual counselor for Charles. His excuse for his next extended absence from work was a terminally ill son. He tried to convince her that he needed to get money to the outside for his son's medical expenses. He wanted her to smuggle a money order for a large amount of money. She could always say that she found the money in her purse at home. In the next few days, Charles said that the baby's condition had worsened, and he was not expected to live. Carol decided that the inmate needed an act of charity, so she signed Charles's money order and even donated a check of her own. At some point, they began to discuss his masculinity. He told her that his wife had divorced him because of his lack of performance. They eventually became sexually involved and were caught. Carol was escorted off the grounds. During an ensuing investigation, Charles pled not guilty and claimed that Carol had paid him one hundred dollars for sexual favors, and he could prove it. Charles' prostitute wife produced the signed money order by Carol who had put it in an envelope with her return address. Even though the employee had included a note showing genuine concern for inmate's imaginary child, she illegally mailed a letter and was discovered in a compromising situation with an inmate; her employment was terminated.

Case History #3

Employee – A white 29 year old stocky man of medium build. He was a Cook Supervisor, worked eight years in prison, and was extremely racially prejudiced. His name was Jim and was married with two children.

Inmate- His name was Ross. He was a white supremacy gang leader and did not possess good work habits. He was sociopathic and could not function well with other people.

Jim felt that Affirmative Action had failed him racially. He confided to Ross about racial minorities being hired in prison and on the street, yet whites always failed to be hired for good jobs. Jim told Ross, "We white boys have to stick together." Inmates, schooled in street psychology, are well aware of the destructive power of hate and use it to their advantage. Jim and Ross' hatred for minorities allowed them to form a special bond. Ross noticed that Jim would always give special treatment to whites when he supervised them. Jim gave cigarettes to Ross and smuggled racially prejudiced magazines against minorities. Rumors began to circulate about Jim being a storm trooper for the American Nazi Party. Minority inmates became angry about the rumors against Jim. As a result, a minority inmate refused to take an order from him. Jim said that he was going to have him locked up. The inmate assumed a fighting stance and challenged the cook to "get it on." The inmate was a large weight lifter and blocked the door way. Ross and a friend of his stepped in front of the inmate in defense of Jim. Peace was restored. Ross told Jim that as long as he was around, no one was going to hurt him. In return, Jim brought packages to him. One day in the kitchen vegetable room, Jim noticed Ross' communication with some minority inmates. Ross was evasive when Jim inquired about their conversation. He had an odd, commanding tone to his voice. They both then stepped inside the vegetable room and all work stopped. The inmates held up their knives, and Jim saw Ross slam the door. The minority inmates circled Jim brandishing their knives in a threatening manner.

As they were closing in, the group stopped when Ross said, "We're friends aren't we, Jim? Friends do friends' favors, don't they? We need a favor, Jim. All we want to do is have a party. We need some way to release our tensions. We could riot, but people get hurt in riots. We don't want to hurt anyone, so you can prevent a riot and you will be a hero." Jim wanted to know how. Ross demanded two bottles of booze when he came to work the next day. To no avail, Jim pled with him because he knew he would lose his job. Ross reminded Jim that everyone was a witness to the racially prejudiced magazines that were smuggled. He also reminded him of the contraband cigarettes. Ross told Jim to bring the booze the next day and place it behind the storage bin. They then would let Jim go with no future favors.

Jim was quiet and sullen and "snapped" at members of his family. He would not tell his wife what was wrong or explain why he had written a $25 check. As he was told, Jim placed the contraband behind the storage bin. He was worried, but he remembered that Ross had told him that no more requests of this nature would be made. He had a gnawing feeling in the pit of his stomach.

Ross didn't report to work for three days. Jim was not about to report him. When Ross did come to work, he had a shopping list of items he wanted. Jim knew he was couldn't refuse. Prison officials became suspicious of Jim's sudden personality change and his worried expression. He was placed under surveillance and arrested when he placed the contraband behind the storage bin. The inmates had "hooked" him and he could not escape their demands.

Case History #4

Employee-Benito, a 35 year-old Italian, who was promoted to Correctional Counselor and had been employed for 4 years. He was known as a fair, but firm supervisor with a college degree. He was short and stocky.

Inmate- Mario was a 23 years old Italian in prison for murder. He had a fourth grade education and was not viewed as a behavioral problem. He was medium build and average height. He was respectful to staff, a hard worker, and active in prison sports.

Benito was assigned to a housing unit of 125 inmates. When inmates complained about rules, Benito began overlooking minor rule violations. As a counselor, Benito had become soft, and inmates immediately perceived this.

Mario approached Benito about working for him, and Benito hired him. He proved to be an excellent worker, and the two men liked each other. They discussed current events, personal problems, and their girlfriends. Benito even started smuggling Mario packs of cigarettes in his cell. When Mario failed to report to work, Benito went to his cell.

Benito said that it was out of character for Mario to be idle. Mario appeared sullen and depressed. He was not receptive to Benito. Mario's eyes never left the wall, nor changed his position on the bed. Finally, Benito told Mario to come to his office so that they could talk more freely. Mario lost his composure and, with tears in his eyes, told Benito that his mother had died. Mario said that his mother never knew he was in prison because he had given her a fictitious address and lied to her about a job he had in the city. In addition, he had a younger sister with no one to care for her. She was arriving on a plane the next day expecting to live with him. No one would be at the airport to greet her. What was he to do? Benito offered a solution. He would be at the airport, and she could stay at his house a few days until they could work out a better solution. Benito told Mario to mention this to no one as he was not supposed to board inmates' relatives. Mario assured him that he would not say a word.

Benito greeted 18 year old Sophia at the airport. She was attractive and appeared much older and experienced than her years. He offered his home to her until they could determine a more permanent solution. When Benito was at work, Sophia washed his clothes, cleaned his house, and cooked his meals. Benito began to perceive affection for Sophia, and he even intended to tell Mario that he had developed a relationship with his sister.

When Benito attempted to contact Mario, he was told he was in the visiting center with his ex-wife. On his way past the admission desk, he glanced at the guest register and saw Mario's name and Rosa's name (his ex-wife). Yet, SOPHIA was sitting in the visitors' center with Mario. There had to be some mistake! There wasn't a mistake, and Mario commanded Benito to sit down. Sophia, Rosa, or whoever she was, had not spoken a word. She looked cold, calculating, and angry. Then Mario pulled out a list from his pocket and demanded Benito to smuggle the following: Percodan, Benzedrine, and Hydrocodone. Benito was astounded and refused.

Sophia (or Rosa) finally spoke up and said, "Listen, you dumb bastard! You'll do it or you won't have a job." Rosa told Benito to get the drugs, or she would tell the warden that she was living with him.

The following day, Benito was caught smuggling drugs into the visiting room and was fired.

Case History # 5

This was a real story about my relatives who owned a car dealership. A very short, soft-spoken man in his sixties who had long blond hair named Roy Rule (real name) came into their dealership and wanted to buy a car. He picked it out but wanted to take it home to show his wife before he purchased it. They trusted him, but he never returned. A few months later, my relatives read in the paper that he and his son had committed armed robbery in a bank in Bakersfield, California. The getaway car was the same stolen car from my relatives, no less. He served three or four years prison time in California. Some years later, Roy returned to the same dealership and told them that he had "Found the Lord" and was so sorry that he had stolen their car. He said that he was honest now and wanted to buy another car. He picked one out and wanted to take it home to show his wife AGAIN. They were so impressed by his honesty, they let him do that. They haven't heard from him since.

Criminals' minds operate on the theory of "Get something for nothing." Prison is just a place to have time to perfect that theory. Sometimes Correctional employees get a "gut-feeling" that something is wrong or that "There is something in the air." Yet, other employees, sadly enough, are "suckered" into the manipulation and suffer criminal consequences.

MICHAEL A. NORCROSS

A log cabin made by an inmate out of rolled paper

A cigarette case made by an inmate out of toothpicks.

A jewelry box made by an inmate out of popsicle sticks

Chapter 26
THE OBSERVANCE OF THE VERNA STAFFORD PAROLE HEARING

The Verna Stafford story was an infamous Oklahoma criminal case that received nationwide publicity. I was employed at OSR during her parole hearing. About once a year, the Oklahoma Department of Corrections holds parole hearings for inmates across the state. Many times OSR sponsored these hearings because we had the biggest gym in the prison system. The waiting inmates filled the gym and would be escorted to the back door of the gym when the parole board was ready for each one. Then each one went into the education building next to the gym where the parole hearing would be conducted.

Verna Stafford was present for parole at one of these hearings at OSR. She and her husband, Roger Stafford, had been convicted of two different crimes in 1978. Roger's brother, Harold, would have been convicted also, but he was killed in a motorcycle accident before the trial began. Their first murders were along Interstate 35 near Purcell, Oklahoma. The Staffords had their car parked on the shoulder of the road with the hood of the car raised. In a deceptive manner, Verna peered under the hood as if she were having car trouble. The Melvin Lorenz family from San Antonio, Texas, drove by and proceeded to assist Verna. When Mr. Lorenz approached the car to see if he could help, Roger and Harold appeared from the ditch and demanded Mr. Lorenz give them his money. Mr. Lorenz refused, so Roger shot and killed him. Mrs. Lorenz heard the shot, approached the Staffords' car, and Roger shot and killed her also. A young boy was in the back seat of their car, sensed something was wrong, and started crying. Roger heard his cries, shot, and killed him also. Dead witnesses can't testify in court! Not much of a reward for trying to help somebody!

A few months later, a young man went to pick up his girlfriend at the Sirloin Stockade in south Oklahoma City. No one appeared to be in the restaurant and the door was open. He called the police. They discovered that six employees had been murdered in the meat locker of the restaurant. His girlfriend was alive but later died at a hospital. Dead witnesses can't testify in court! One of the dead employees was a man, and the other five were young students.

It was later revealed that the three criminals had intended to rob the restaurant. In the process, the adult employee angered Roger. The three then herded the victims into the meat locker, shot and killed them. The police later found the gun that had both Verna's and Roger's fingerprints on it. The crime went unsolved for several months until a drunken Roger Stafford called a police dispatcher. He said his brother Harold Stafford had done all of the killings. The police were able to trace the call to Roger and Verna in Chicago. They were then arrested and extradited to Oklahoma. As it so sadly happens sometimes, the media sensationalized the trio.

Roger was convicted and was given the death penalty. He was taken to Death Row at the "Walls" (another name for the Oklahoma State

Penitentiary). I later talked to a Correctional Officer who had to transport Roger. He said he looked at Roger in the back seat through his mirror and the hair on the back of his neck would stand up. Verna had testified against Roger at their trial. An officer who worked on Death Row said that Roger had said that he should have killed the bitch, too, when he had the chance. Roger later died by lethal injection in the death chamber at OSP. A story was rumored about a preacher at that prison who baptized inmates on Death Row. Before he supposedly baptized Roger, the preacher told him that it didn't matter how many people that he killed, he was going to heaven. Roger supposedly said, "If he had known it was that easy to get into heaven, I would have killed more people."

Verna said at her hearing that she couldn't control Roger. Much to her disadvantage, she had insulted one of the parole board members to the media. The member said that as long as he was on the parole board she would never be paroled. She had children who were placed with the Department of Human Services. She said that she wanted them to grow up on a ranch.

Verna was convicted and given a life sentence with the possibility of parole. To my knowledge, she has never made parole, and I personally hope that she never does. I felt she should have received the death penalty.

After the parole hearings in the education building, she came back through to the gym. I was standing about three feet from her, and her presence made the hair on the back of my neck stand up.

MICHAEL A. NORCROSS

Chapter 27
THE LOWEST STATUS IN A PRISON

In American culture, social or professional status seems to be important. Politicians, doctors, lawyers, or college professors obtain their status through education. Sports figures or film actors/actresses obtain their status through publicity and wealth. Many adults and youth envy many of these positions. On the other hand, criminals are categorized as the lowest status in our society, and criminals are even rated among themselves.

Murderers are held in the lowest esteem in our culture. I worked in corrections long enough to know that I could talk to murderers without being nervous or afraid. When I was in high school some forty-nine years ago, I remember a lawyer's son who raped a girl in Oklahoma City. The incident was talked about in schools, stores, and coffee shops. No one could believe that something this atrocious could happen in Oklahoma. It was unheard of for a person of that social/economic standing to commit rape. There were three young girl scouts who were killed at a Girl Scout camp in Locust Grove, Oklahoma, that has gone unsolved. There were two young girls who were killed on a dirt road in Weleetka, Oklahoma, that went unsolved for several years. Investigators have recently charged a man with those murders. Today, because of the media, we know that almost ten murders a week are committed in Oklahoma. We continue to condemn the murderer.

Within the walls of a prison, the child molester/murderer is held on the bottom rung of the ladder among the hierarchy that inmates create for themselves. In prison, just about all child molesters have to "go on protective custody" or be killed by other inmates. The only exception to this that I know of was a man who was convicted on circumstantial evidence. He was well liked and accepted on the yard. Somehow inmates have a way of discovering the nature of the crime of other inmates: watching television, reading newspapers in the law library, or word of mouth. Ironically, prisoners rate other prisoners by the nature of their crime, and the inmates who kill, abuse, or molest a child are of the lowest status.

I know of such circumstances and consequences of child abuse. A baby was seen standing in the middle of the street in Elk City. The weather was extremely cold, and the baby wore only a diaper. The little girl, who was not more than a year old, was crying and freezing. A Probation and Parole Officer wrapped her in his jacket and took her to the police department while he and the chief looked for the parents. They found a man sitting in his back yard whittling wood and asked if a child was in his care. He said that his baby was in the house asleep, so the lost child could not be his. The investigation proved that the child was missing and indeed the one in police care. The caretaker seemed to be unconcerned when told that the baby had been discovered in the middle of the street about a block from his house.

A Probation and Parole Officer searched for a couple who had recently transferred their probation supervision from Arkansas. They were not at the address listed on the transfer papers. It was in the dead of winter with ice on the ground. He finally located their broken down vehicle on the median of Interstate 40. When he finally found their current residence, it was without heat or water. They discovered a small child, clothed only in a diaper that was literally frozen to the floor. The parents were fully clothed and covered while the child was freezing to death. The child was quickly wrapped in a heavy coat and placed in the services at DHS. Sadly enough, the Officer was sure that the parents eventually regained custody of the child.

Many child molesters are never rehabilitated and must always be registered as sex offenders. A sex offender moved to Elk City, Oklahoma, during the Oil Boom. He had difficulty locating and maintaining employment since he was a sex offender. The Probation and Parole Office working the Elk City area was notified of the sexual molestation of two small children who lived in the same area of this sex offender. When the Officer arrived at the offender's residence, a neighbor advised the Officer that the offender had been babysitting the children that morning. Within a few days, the Officer found the child molester in custody in Florida. Witnesses said that after obscenities had been exchanged between the offender and a passerby, the offender had wielded a knife. He was immediately arrested and was found wanted by the State of Oklahoma. When he was returned to Oklahoma, he pled guilty to the offense of Child Molestation and was sentenced to a lengthy prison term.

The worst case of child abuse, molestation, and murder that I had ever heard of was by a man named Richard Norman Rojem. He was convicted in Macomb County, Michigan, in 1979 for the crimes of Criminal Sexual Conduct 1st Degree, 3 counts; and Criminal Sexual Conduct 2nd Degree, Count 4; receiving a sentence of 6 to 15 years with the Michigan Department of Corrections. Once released on parole, he transferred his supervision to the State of Oklahoma in July 1982. He lived with his wife and her two children in Sayre, Oklahoma, where he was employed as an oil field worker. From the beginning, there were indications of on-going problems with Rojem and his wife. On February 3, 1983, a Probation and Parole Officer suspected that there was sexual contact between Rojem, his seven year old step-daughter Layla Cummings, and her brother Jason. The mother brought both of the children to the County Sheriff's Department and a Probation and Parole Officer interviewed them. Layla admitted that Richard Norman Rojem made her get into bed with him. The Officer contacted the Assistant D.A., but he said the girl could not testify in court; therefore, charges would not be filed. Because of the numerous violations against him, Rojem's parole was revoked, and he was returned to Michigan to serve his original sentence. The State of Michigan held Rojem for approximately six months before releasing him again. He returned to Washita County, Oklahoma, because of his employment, but the Officer objected to the return. On July 7, 1984, The Officer was notified that Layla Cummings had been kidnapped from her mother's home in Elk City. The Officer received directions to a wheat field near Burns Flat, Oklahoma. Seven-year-old

Layla Dawn Cummings lay face down in the wheat field in her mother's night gown. She had been abducted from her home in Elk City, taken to this deserted location, raped, and killed. The skin on her buttocks was torn, probably by fingernail scratches. Her panties had been removed and stuffed in her mouth. A farmer had found the body that morning and had notified authorities. Richard Norman Rojem was convicted by a jury in Washita County of first degree rape, kidnapping, and murder of seven-year- old Layla Cummings. He received the death penalty for the murder and 1000 years imprisonment for both the kidnapping and the rape. He has been on death row at the Oklahoma State Penitentiary since that time and files one appeal after another. He is a dangerous sociopath and should have been executed long ago. Many people had rather he die by the electric chair than lethal injection. The Bible says in Matthew 18:6, "Whosoever offends one of these little ones who believes in me it is better that a millstone were hanged around his neck and that he were drowned in the depth of the sea." Those who harm children are definitely the lowest status among other criminals. I'm sure they are considered that appalling by society, in general, as well.

"Old Sparky," this electric chair was used from 1913-1966. Eighty-two Oklahoma inmates were executed by electrocution during this time period. We are hoping that the person in this chapter who raped and killed a little girl will be executed by the electric chair rather than lethal injection since it will more painful.

Chapter 28
A 1973 PRISON RIOT

As long as there are prisons, there will be riots and the Oklahoma Department of Corrections has had its share. A year before I came to work at OSR new units were being built at the prison. The workers kept their tools behind a chain link fence. During a racial altercation among inmates, some inmates managed to steal these tools to use in a "mini-riot." As previously mentioned, during my first years at OSR, there were rumors all year that there would be a riot. At Dick Conner Correctional Center at Hominy, Oklahoma, on August 29, 1983, about 80 inmates went to the chow hall to protest the food. They were joined by additional inmates making a mob. Orders were given for the inmates to return to their housing units, but they were ignored. A rock was thrown through a kitchen window, and the acts of destruction escalated into a full scale riot. The inmates torched the buildings adjacent to the kitchen and completely destroyed the library, school, and church area. One inmate died and $3 million dollars' worth of damage ensued. In September 1983, the Legislature appropriated $2.5 million dollars to fund the reconstruction of Dick Conner Correctional Center.

One of the state's worst riots occurred at the Oklahoma State Penitentiary at McAlester in 1973. After this prison riot, many of the inmates were transferred to OSR. I learned about the riot from inmates who witnessed it. One inmate told me that he was working in the kitchen and was privy to the impending riot. Because he respected his staff supervisor, the inmate told him NOT to report to work the next day. The employee heeded his word, and it probably saved his life.

The afternoon of July 27, 1973, was probably not the target date for the riot but takeover plans had been formulated for some time. Deputy Warden Sam Johnson later was made aware that the riot had been planned for months. Prison officials were mindful of its severity and had told numerous people that they needed help. The yards were crowded that afternoon with hundreds of idle inmates, many drunk, glued up, or high on some type of drug. An inmate told me he overheard partial conversations among fifteen inmates who tried to recruit others to join them. The instigators suggested killing half a dozen of the prison employees and taking the others hostage while some argued against hurting anyone. At about 2:30 P.M. the group proceeded to the inmate mess hall where they attacked two Officers. Both men were hospitalized with stab wombs. Six or seven armed inmates started taking hostages. The first call over the public address system reported, "We're taking over. We've got weapons. We've got hostages. It's a revolution. Come on and help us."

There was a full scale riot in progress. Using homemade knives and other weapons, rioting inmates kicked correctional Officers and kitchen personnel. Ironically, some of the hostage-taking was apparently perpetrated for the protection of certain prison personnel. Several hostages reported being "protected" from hostile inmates. One correctional Officer said that one convict held a knife to his throat, kissed him on the ear, and said,

"Nobody will mess with you." Other hostages didn't fare so well. One Officer who ran to the rescue of an inmate cook was badly beaten by rioting inmates who broke his glasses and clubbed him 35 times. From 2:30 until 4:00, many people were reported unconscious or badly beaten. An inmate who went to the mess hall later described the carnage. He said there was blood all over the tables. It reminded him of a butcher shop. Ten human beings could not have shed more blood if they been drawn and quartered.

The key hostage during most of the riot was the Deputy Warden. As the afternoon progressed, many inmates found stashes of homemade beer and other intoxicants. Some looted the medical supplies in the hospital area and ingested any kind of drug available. Others spent time in the paint shop, sniffing glue and paint thinner, which served only to worsen the problems. Even innocent inmates had to protect themselves from the more violent rioters. For employee hostage safety, the inmates forced these employees to dress as inmates. This disguise protected at least two employees hidden by friendly inmates. Since the rioting inmates didn't know these employees on sight, they believed them to be other prisoners.

The first of three casualties occurred at 4:30 P.M. when three inmates entered the West Cell House, took an inmate to the male clothing area, stabbed him repeatedly, and beat him to death. A "body" reportedly lay on the yard for several hours. At the end of the riot, the body was gone. There were many people lying on the ground faking death, and some of the rioting inmates assumed them to be dead. By 5:35 P.M., the hospital had been seized, additional hostages taken, bringing the number of hostages to fourteen. By 6:00 P.M. all of the buildings in the north side of the security area were burning. The print shop, chapel, library, and sign plant were destroyed. The plasma clinic, book bindery, broom and mattress factory, bakery, and mess hall were burning. All of the industrial area was either destroyed or burning. Inmates roamed everywhere except the main administration area. At 6:20 P.M. the hospital was burning. By 7:30 P.M. the canteen was burning. Twenty-one officers were held hostage. To complicate matters further, telephone service was severely impeded because inmates had seized an outside telephone line in the firehouse and were placing calls all over the country.

The Oklahoma National Guard mobilized the 180th Infantry. For several hours, the only source of light was that of burning buildings. The cover of darkness further discouraged officers from searching the compound for hostages. Many inmates used the darkness as an opportunity to take revenge on fellow inmates that they despised. More buildings were torched, and inmates threatened to burn New Cell House F, which would also have doomed the Rotunda. Inmates looted cell houses, and at 12:45 A.M. an inmate was stabbed to death by another inmate in the East Cell House. Hundreds of inmates tried to storm Tower 8 with Molotov cocktails. The firebombing of Tower 8 prompted officials to make contact with guards in that tower and in Tower 11. The men in those towers had received no relief, no food or water, and no radio communication for at least ten hours after the riot had begun. It was believed that inmates had ladders and were planning to scale the wall at Tower 8, then guards from Tower 8 fired shots into the crowd. After midnight many of the rowdy inmates were unconscious from drunkenness or drug induced sleep. Even though there were death and destruction all around them, a group of inmates played basketball in the recreation area. There was talk of the National Guard storming the compound, but the Deputy Warden knew that it would be a literal inferno. Inmates had saturated blankets with hot grease to make the floors slippery and there were 10 gallons of naphtha and 100 Molotov cocktails. Four hostages were released at 8:30P.M. At 10:40 P.M., a group of 150 to 200 inmates surrendered at the West Gate. Ambulances hurried injured prisoners to hospitals. The Governor had ongoing negotiations with an inmate picked by the Deputy Warden. An onslaught of media caused problems for the investigation. At 12:30 P.M., all of the hostages had been freed. At 1:00 P.M., convicts charged the Administration Building and set fire to the northeast cell block. Officials believed the new outbreak was caused by inmates looking for informers.

Oklahoma Highway Patrol troopers and National Guardsmen entered the prison at 9:30 A.M. on Sunday to sweep the compound for bodies, weapons, or hiding inmates. An additional 1,000 guardsmen were called to OSP to relieve those who had been on duty since the riot's inception. The following Sunday, August 5, the last guardsmen left. There were many reasons for the riot: overcrowding, refusal of the Governor to sign parole recommendations, understaffing caused by poor correctional officer wage ($380 a month), inmate abuse, continued racial segregation, censorship, poor health care, poor food, idleness, and better recreation which get extremely better. The State of Oklahoma found itself under years of federal court order.

The OSP riot changed the face of Oklahoma Corrections forever. Just about all DOC officials think that the riot made improved changes for the Department.

Oklahoma State Penitentiary is the only maximum security prison in Oklahoma.

Buildings burning at the 1973 riot

Officer standing guard at the 1973 riot

MICHAEL A. NORCROSS

Chapter 29
A 1980 PRISON RIOT

Time magazine called the 1980 New Mexico riot, "The nation's most notorious prison riot in history." The terror lasted for thirty-six hours. When it was over, thirty-three inmates were dead: all at the hands of their fellow convicts. It was an outbreak of prison violence unequaled in the annals of prison uprisings.

After the riot, about thirty-five New Mexico inmates were sent to OSR and to the rest of the country. I remember that one of the inmates we received had been badly beaten. Most of the information about the riot that I received came from an Officer who had read about it. Some of the information came from a New Mexico Officer who relocated inmates to OSR. The inmates we received had issues concerning food and recreation. After the riot, the State of New Mexico implemented many new correctional policies, including more diverse recreation.

The New Mexico Department of Corrections had a history of riots. In 1950 there was another riot between inmates and guards. There was an unsuccessful escape attempt in 1952 when a guard was killed and a warden resigned. However, the New Mexico legislature did not take immediate action. The new penitentiary was opened April 20, 1956, with the usual public relations ribbon-cutting ceremony. The legislature touted it as a model of humane corrections, and the state bragged about the $24,000 spent on the gas chamber. In 1958, the Governor cited a problem with inmate idleness. (In

1956, a guard's starting salary was $265 a month; in 1980, it was $765 a month.)

On Friday, February 1, 1980, an inmate saw a full moon from his cell window, an omen to him as he had read a full moon increases crime. He wasn't aware that a full-scale prison riot was impending. (The original plan revolved around a show that the local university radio station was to broadcast from the prison gymnasium. They planned to take the D.J. hostage and use the broadcasting facilities to communicate to the public about the prison's conditions. This plan was aborted.) Eight inmates had ingested home brew made of fermented raisins, yeast, sugar, and water. In their drunken stupor, they sat around the table in the day room of their dormitory.

Two officers arrived at 1:30 A.M. to close the day room and get the count. When they left, they accidentally left the door ajar. The inmates assaulted the two officers, dragged them into the day room, stripped them naked, bound their ankles with torn bed sheets, and blindfolded them. The inmates repeatedly stomped, kicked, punched, and spit on the officers. One of the rioters stole a captain's uniform and his keys to open all of the doors to the cells of the general population inmates. Within fifteen minutes, five hundred inmates were freed and had weapons: legs broken off metal tables and beds, knives, razors, broken jars, and anything else they could find. The Protection Unit secured their doors with chairs, tables, and beds.

About 2:00 A.M., an inmate heard a mob yelling and screaming. He looked out his cell window and saw about one hundred inmates running to the central control booth dragging a half-crawling, naked, blindfolded Officer with a rope around his neck. They were kicking him in the ribs and whacking his legs. The rioters took over the control room, which is the nerve center of any prison. They forced entry to the riot gear and distributed riot helmets, bombs, batons, and gas masks. Seventy-five inmates began the riot, but their number greatly increased. Every record in classification was burned. The reveling and rioting inmates had free access to phones. People in New York became privy to the riot before the citizens in Santa Fe, which was eleven miles away. Many inmates burglarized the pharmacy and took advantage of all its drugs and paraphernalia.

One target of the rioters was "The Dog," the biggest snitch in the prison. He had snitched on most of the inmates in Cell block 3, and they wanted revenge. He attempted to jam his cell door with a toothbrush. The inmates found an acetylene cutting torch and dragged it upstairs to the protection unit. They cut the metal on his cell door, and it came off its hinges. They dragged him out of his cell and handcuffed his arms and legs spread eagle to the bars in front of the guard station block. They wanted to make him a public example of torture and execution. His screams could be heard throughout the prison. They beat him with riot sticks and chains, breaking his legs, knocking his teeth out, bloodying his face, and hammering his chest and stomach. The beating was so intense that he passed out, but one of the execution squad members found smelling salts to bring him to consciousness. Taking a straight razor, they slit the skin over both eye lids and gouged out his eye balls until they hung down on his cheeks. When they fell to the floor, he begged for the execution squad to kill him, but they wouldn't. His body was so mutilated that it took many hours to reveal his identity.

One of the rioters attacked another snitch, hit him with a riot stick, drew blood, and knocked him to the ground. They attacked him mercilessly with their pipes and clubs, kicking and beating him. After they tied a rope under his arms and around his chest, they hung him from the rafters on the basketball court for all to see. During those hours of craziness, inmates hacked at his dangling corpse with knives, beat it with pipes, and mutilated it beyond recognition. His body was a raw bloody mass of flesh by the time that the uprising was over.

At 5:00 a.m. the psychological building was burning, and the rioters made the band room the command post. The Governor, Deputy Warden of Corrections, and the Warden had arrived and threatened to send in the SWAT team. The National Guard was on its way. A Muslim Minister said the blacks did not participate in the riot and wouldn't interfere with them. A minister tried to save one mentally ill inmate in his cell, but the squad grabbed him by his hair, sawed through his neck, severed skin, bone, and muscle until his head rolled off his body. The raping and executions continued. Eighty inmates, thought to be dead in the gymnasium, were unconscious from drugs. Two National Guard helicopter medical support teams arrived and evacuated the more seriously injured to hospitals. The inmate negotiators gave a list of their demands to the Governor. Some were granted and others denied. One demand was improvement of recreational facilities. One National Guardsman told reporters that he had been in Vietnam two years but never had experienced the carnage that he did at this riot.

After thirty-six hours, the bloodiest prison riot in the nation's history ended. Thirty-three inmates were dead, hundreds hospitalized, and many more were mentally and emotionally traumatized. One anthropologist and other specialists were recruited to identify fragments of human bones in the ashes and rubble that covered the burned out gym floor. However, the riot had not ended for the relatives of the inmates and employees. They were still standing at the front tower waiting to see if their loved ones were dead or alive.

By Thursday, February 7, some 496 inmates were in dormitories that were habitable. 470 inmates were transferred to other prisons in Oklahoma, Kansas, and Georgia. The legislature passed an emergency bill authorizing $87.5 million dollars to be spent on the prison system.

One of the reasons for the riot was believed to have been the head of the psychological unit. Inmates held a bitter disdain for this man who probably had landed about every inmate in the Hole at least once. (The Hole was located in the basement under Cell block 3 and just behind death row. Naked inmates were secluded with only a thin blanket, a toothbrush, and a metal cup. They were fed a meal every three days and six slices of bread on days in between.) He did not like psychiatrists and had no use for psychotropic medication. Many inmates he had counseled committed suicide. He developed one of the most bizarre procedures in prison history. A plaster body cast was put on the inmate from neck to ankles with holes for defecation and urination. This was developed in 1978 as an "alternative to drug therapy." He said that it was more humane to physically restrain people for their own safety than administer tranquilizers, even though an inmate was tranquilized to fit the body cast. The psychologist obviously had a "character disorder" as outlined in the Mental Health manual.

Another reason for the riot was availability of drugs. Most of the inmates in Cellblock 5 stayed high on some kind of drug seven days a week. Drugs were readily available as there was always some underpaid guard eager to make a fast buck and ready to supply whatever drug desired. A bag of grass which cost $25 would sell for $150 to the inmate. Cell block 5 always had a steady supply of home brew. In 1973, bikers from the west coast were smuggling drugs across country. When incarcerated, they tried to start a chapter of the American Nazi Chapter in the penitentiary.

Regardless the cause, the misery in the prison continued after the riot as inmates claimed they were beaten by guards as revenge for the riot. A new director for the Department of Corrections was in the process of building five new facilities. He wanted the entire system to be transformed into a "Corrections College" that would recondition and educate every inmate. The inmates would be the students, and the employees would be the instructors. There would be conjugal visits, not only with wives, but also with girlfriends. Yoga would be used with hard core inmates. His was yet ANOTHER philosophy of rehabilitating criminals.

In 1787, Ben Rush proposed to Benjamin Franklin in Philadelphia that the correct way to treat offenders was to insist on repentance of their crimes. In 1825, Elam Lynds, the first warden of Sing Sing, said "Reformation of the criminal could not possibly be affected until the spirit of the criminal is broken." In 1826, The North Carolina Supreme Court said, "To know right and still pursue wrong proceeds from a perverse wit brought about by the seductions of the Evil One." In the 1930's, a German attested that men who were stout and squat with large abdomens were usually the occasional offender. Men with slight muscular build were usually the habitual offender. In 1870 and even now poverty is the main factor is the making of a criminal. There have always been and will continue to be many theories for the behavior of criminals, but no one really has an answer.

MICHAEL A. NORCROSS

Chapter 30
BIZZARE STORIES ABOUT INMATES, PROBATIONERS, AND PAROLEES

Through the years with the Oklahoma Department of Corrections, I had the opportunity to exchange stories with inmates, staff, or Probation and Parole Officers in the area other than my work in recreation. However, some of these stories were Officers who worked at the gym. Most of these stories concerned the crimes that inmates committed or the behavior of inmates or parolees. Some crimes were not necessarily serious in nature, but were bizarre. These stories make for interesting reading. I hope that the reader is not faint of heart. Most of these crime stories were blue-collar crimes. However, many inmates specialized in their crimes. Regardless of the type or specialty of crime, the stories were definitely peculiar.

One inmate specialized in robbing only convenience stores with a shotgun; he never used a pistol or a rifle. Another inmate, who was Indian, always spoke with a Mexican accent in the execution of his robberies. (After he was discharged from prison, I saw him on the street and asked him what he was currently doing. He replied that he didn't have to do anything because he had married a woman who could make a good living for him.)

Of course, only a murderer can understand the mindset of another murderer and understand why the following inmates might have acted accordingly. One inmate killed a person and thought that he might be able to use the body later, so he put the body in the trunk of his car. He got his car stuck on a muddy road, got the body out of the trunk, and put it under one of the tires for traction. One inmate got his hair cut, went home, looked in the mirror and didn't like the way the barber cut it. He returned to the barber shop and cut off all of the barber's fingers. One murderer was afraid that the police would find his victim, so he cut the body up and put it into a suitcase. Two inmates buried their murdered victim, was afraid he might be found, and reburied it. However, the body was eventually found. An inmate, who killed two people, put their bodies in an incinerator to conceal their identity, but the Medical Examiner identified them from the bones. The murderer was convicted and sent to prison. "Ice Cream Man" drove an ice cream truck on the street. He enticed a young girl into his truck, took her to the country, and beat her to death with a pop bottle. He was convicted and sent to Joe Harp Correctional Center. His young son came to visit him in the visiting room. He intentionally burned him with a cigarette. Because other inmates witnessed the act, he was sent to Protective Custody at OSR; he soon hung himself in his cell. Beside his body was a picture of Charlie Brown and Peanuts eating ice cream cones.

Officers have their own stories when dealing with inmates. Many years before I came to work at OSR, there was an Officer named "Scoot" Nickell who was a very large man with a short-fuse. He always carried a pair of brass knuckles and was known to use them. Yet, he was a good Officer and a good man. One inmate, drunk on home brew, refused to return to his cell and tried to hit another Officer with a mop handle. Without hesitation, "Scoot" knocked him unconscious with a pick handle.

I felt some employees acted as bizarrely as some inmates. Jack Plummer was a psychologist at OSR and was a strange character. He enjoyed barbequed goat and served it at his parties. He was always conducting some kind of experiment. He once set up a series of mirrors at the prison hog farm to monitor their reactions at seeing themselves. The experiment burned the hog barn to the ground. The sun reflected on one of the mirrors at just the right angle, started a fire, and all of the hogs were lost.

If inmates are released before their sentence is completely served, they are entrusted to a Probation and Parole Officer on the outside for the remainder of their time. These Officers meet with their assigned inmate periodically in and out of the inmate's residence. These Officers can relate some uncanny tales. One Probation and Parole Officer investigated a burglary at the Blue Front Bar in Harmon County. The back room's entrance was covered with a hanging blanket. Inside the room, the Officer found a human fetus in a five-gallon jar. The fetus was approximately five months developed and had probably been delivered still-born. The owner of the bar was charging his customers ten cents a person to view the contents of the jar.

An Officer made a routine home visit to an individual in Hollis, Oklahoma. After knocking on the door, he quickly stepped back because of an infestation of flies. The screen door was black with them. When he opened the door, thousands of flies escaped from the residence. A woman was sitting in a chair with a half-eaten watermelon in her lap. Her hair, face, arms, and legs were covered with flies. He noticed a heavily, padlocked log chain around her refrigerator. She said the locked chain was necessary to keep her children from stealing her food.

An Officer had received a tip that one of his Probationers had a grenade in his house. He and the Chief of Police went to search the home, and they detected an odor inside the bedroom. A two hundred fifty pound pig was being raised in the house.

One of the most savage and senseless robberies in Western Oklahoma's history occurred in Gould, Oklahoma, a little town in Harmon County. Two men walked into the bank and declared a robbery. One of the male workers was pistol whipped and two female tellers were kidnapped, taken to the country, shot, and left for dead. One of the female tellers died; the other dragged herself to the road and was found by the rural mail carrier. The robbers immediately went to Hollis, about 10 minutes away, and started spending the stolen money at a local store. Both men were quickly captured and imprisoned. One of them was killed while in custody.

PCP was one of the most widely used drugs in the 1960's through the 1980's. It could be an anesthetic, stimulant, depressant, or hallucinogen, often causing violent and unpredictable behavior, coma, seizures, and death. A woman, high on PCP, was caught directing traffic in Elk City, Oklahoma. When she was arrested, she was fighting, cursing, swinging wildly, and screaming. The only way the Officers could contain her in a cell was to choke her until she passed out.

One of the most difficult issues for a Probation and Parole Officer to face is a family destroyed by substance abuse. One Officer was assigned to an alcoholic who had lost his family, self-respect, job, home, and seemingly his future. One afternoon, the Officer and his partner returned home from a training session and made a home visit at the man's mobile home. When their knocking didn't arouse the man, they peered through the window and saw several bottles of Lysol lying on the floor. The parolee was seen lying on the floor unconscious from the ingestion of the Lysol. Somehow the man survived.

Many Probation and Parole Officers work with mentally ill individuals. Some are psychotic, paranoid, or hallucinatory. One Officer had a parolee who thought he could literally see the electricity running from the electrical outlet into the floor. Another Officer had a parolee who fired shots at him. When the Officer came to take him into custody to be hospitalized, an FBI agent aimed to fire at him before he knew the man was mentally ill. After the guns were lowered and the parolee stopped firing, the parolee literally lifted the front of the police car from the ground. He was not taking his prescribed medications.

Paint sniffers are sometimes called "huffers." They are volatile and can be dangerous. These people become addicted to gasoline, glue, paint thinner, or any other kind of toxic compound. Many people who have sniffed substances for years have irreversible brain damage. There was an inmate at OSR that everyone called Burn Out. I don't think his circuits were burned out, and oddly enough, everyone liked him.

A Probation and Parole Officer was assigned to a "hardcore huffer." He would sniff anything, but his drug of choice was gold spray paint. Many times the Officer would contact him, and he would have gold paint around his mouth or in his nostrils. Another Officer observed a driver in another car with a plastic bag over his nose and mouth. When the Officer attempted an arrest, the driver was passed out in the middle of the highway.

One Probationer in Mangum, Oklahoma, was having problems with family, finances, and employment. His wife called authorities and said that he had run her and her children out of the house. He had barricaded himself in the house, was taking all the inside doors off their hinges, and nailing them over the windows inside the house. When authorities questioned him about his behavior, he said that he was just having a "bad day."

An Officer inquired about the whereabouts of a parolee at his eighty-five year old grandmother's residence. As the Officer left the residence, he was admiring her tomatoes, beets, cantaloupes, okra, and beans in her garden. He then noticed the tops of the tomato vines were ragged and discovered that there were marijuana plants growing between each tomato plant. The woman admitted growing the marijuana plants. She even showed the Officer two aluminum pans under her bed which contained drying marijuana. She said that she was selling it to supplement her social security check. The Officer took the contraband and told her not to grow any more marijuana.

There was a parolee with transferred supervision to Oklahoma who was known as the "panty thief." For several months there had been someone in Sayre, Oklahoma, breaking into residences and taking only women's panties. Many women in the county were scared and afraid to stay home alone. The State of Texas had issued a parole revocation warrant and a Probation and Parole Officer went to his residence to arrest him. When he was booked into the county jail, he was wearing several pairs of women's panties.

A Probation and Parole Officer received a call that there was a man standing naked on Interstate-40. The man was watching the traffic and enjoying an occasional honk, whistle, or wave. Before a sheriff's deputy arrested him, the deputy inquired about his behavior. The man said, "Well, I'm crazy."

Two Probation and Parole Officers went to a house after talking to neighbors who said a man was experiencing mental problems. They said that he had been up all night practicing marital arts and had been breaking out windows in his house. They discovered that the man was a physician. His diploma was displayed in a frame on his wall. All over the living room were various surgical instruments, medical books, and other medical publications. In one of the medical journals was a section marked and underlined dealing with appendectomies. The man had drawn a diagram on his side with a marker; he was about to remove his own appendix. The Probationer was taken to a Mental Health facility.

An inmate high on drugs in Oklahoma City, was hungry, and had little money. Instead of taking that money and buying food, he bought a gun. He robbed Crab Shack in Bricktown in broad daylight. Most inmates do not think things out before they act. He was convicted, sent to OSR, and placed on Protection. He said he was a reformed homosexual.

Inmates have told me that if interrupted during a burglary, they had no choice but to commit murder. Even though they did not want to kill, they felt compelled to because, "A dead witness can't testify." An inmate once said to me, "We aren't in here for singing too loud in church."

MICHAEL A. NORCROSS

Chapter 31
INTERESTING ODDS AND ENDS

The Oklahoma Penal System embraces diverse history throughout the years. At one time the only two facilities were the Oklahoma State Reformatory and the Oklahoma State Penitentiary. This was before any recreation programs had been implemented. Their early stories about inmate labor, inmate population, medical treatment, and employee regulations are noteworthy.

Inmates have been used for labor in some form of public domain for years. During World War II, the OSR inmate work gangs, under armed security guards, assisted local farmers with the harvest of cotton and feed crops. Cotton was picked or pulled and feed bundled by hand. The counties contracted with the state for convict labor and, in return, agreed to pay transportation costs and the difference in the keep of the prisoners. This cost included food, medical attention, guards, and any cost incurred in recapturing escapees. However, the use of convict gangs benefited the counties and the state at the expense of the prison and the inmates. Each gang had from 20 to 100 convicts, two to six guards, a steward, and a foreman. At one time, the prison had over 300 men working in nine counties. Using mule teams, the inmates worked without wages from dawn to dusk to clear roadways. They slept in collapsible tents and were transferred from county to county. Because the escape rate was high, extra guards were necessary; thus, the cost of this contract soared draining the prison budget.

Road building became a big business after World War II; therefore, inmate gang labor ceased.

Conditions at the prisons changed dramatically with the onset of World War II. Because prison goods weren't being produced and sold, inmates were idle. This changed in October 1942 as OSP received a quarter of a million dollars in contracts for Navy clothing, furniture, rope, and bricks. By the end of 1943, the board of public Welfare reported to the Governor that it had accepted well over a half-million dollars of military contracts for the year.

Inmate population is an ongoing issue. From its inception, Oklahoma's incarceration rate has been excessive. Between 1909 and 1935 the combined average monthly inmate population increased from 718 to 3,656, more than 500 percent. In 1936, Oklahoma had only 2 percent of the nation's population, but it had over 3 percent of the nation's prison population. From 1935 to 1937, the prison population increased 12 percent from 3,200 to 3,600 inmates and reached a high of 4,000 in 1937. Oklahoma prison's population doubled between the 1920's and 1930's. It exceeded prison capacity by twenty-five percent. The penitentiary warden pleaded for more cell space because, in 1930, he had two to three hundred inmates sleeping in corridors. Therefore, idleness became a major problem in state prisons during the 1930's. The only employment for most inmates was make-work tasks. More than 40 percent of the prisoners performed menial maintenance functions. The rest of the population was either sick or unemployed. A study team said that it was important to keep the inmates busy.

Between 1981 and 1986, the incarceration rate again nearly doubled in Oklahoma prisons, which placed Oklahoma tenth in the nation. Regionally, Oklahoma and Texas were the leaders in incarceration. Oklahoma was second in 1981, but in 1986, Oklahoma surpassed Texas. Most crimes in Oklahoma were non-violent; the highest categories were drug and DUI offenses.

At the end of 1927, Warden John Newell reported a population of 2,370 males and 61 females. The next year he reported the population at 2,937, an increase of 262 prisoners in one year. The penitentiary had nine sentenced to death, 366 for life, 391 for terms ranging from five to ten years, eight held for safe keeping, and the remainder for terms ranging from two months to four years and eleven months

The first prison hospital was built at OSP in the 1920's. This building was replaced by a new hospital in 1956, which is still standing. The original hospital building was destroyed during the prison riot in 1973. Before medical units were implemented, inmate "doctors" performed surgical procedures. One of the most infamous of these inmate doctors was Buster Higgins. He served time in the 30's and 40's. He committed suicide in the mid 40's in the X-ray room of the new hospital. To benefit pharmaceutical companies, a medical doctor named Austin Stough established a "guinea pig" program for testing new medication on inmates at OSP. He eventually increased his staff, primarily with former military corpsmen, and they began to compile medical records on inmates. He later started a plasmapheresis program and inmates could donate their blood for money. He left the prison system because of political difficulties. State law now prohibits inmates from donating blood.

During the early 1900's, the daily menu at the penitentiary and the reformatory was one piece of meat, gravy or syrup, bread, and coffee for breakfast. The noon meal included a meat, potato, maybe a green vegetable, and bread. The meat portion for the evening meal varied depending on the availability of beef. If there were no leftovers to make a stew, the inmates received a bowl of rice, tomatoes, or prunes, with bread and water, and maybe some coffee. Desserts, such as bread pudding or pie, were usually served on Saturday.

Gaining dependable, competent employees has remained a challenge for the penal system. Selection of prison personnel on the basis of political influence and low wages increased the problems of under qualified staff. One Warden said in 1913, "They are, I believe, as competent as you can get men to work for $60 a month." Salaries inched up during the next thirty years, but remained well below subsistent wages. During the war years of the 1940's, wage inflation and the availability of jobs in the war industries robbed the prisons of able employees. Warden Hunt in the early 1940's proposed a raise of $12.50 per month to bring the prison guard wage to $112.50 a month. The Navy ammunitions depot at McAlester offered jobs at $3 a day. Prison jobs paid only $100 a month. A $25 a month raise came only after more than a dozen prison employees quit their jobs during a two week period.

In the beginning, guards worked 12-hour shifts, seven days a week on a staggered schedule of one month of days followed by a month of nights. This was later changed to a schedule of bimonthly shift changes that continued into the late 1950's. The guards inside the cell houses worked eight-hour shifts, but the horse-mounted guards who patrolled the work gangs outside the walls worked twelve hour shifts from "early morning to late afternoon." These long hours violated state law, which limited public employees to an eight-hour work day, but the prisons ignored the law for their guards. The employees had 44 rules to obey in the prison rule book, which included not discussing prison business! The inmates had only 23 rules! The guards worked seven days a week until the mid-1950's when the work week was reduced to six days. The guards continued to work a minimum of sixty hours a week and up to eighty-four hours in case of an emergency.

A legislative committee in 1957 reported that seventy percent of all prison employees earned less than $190 a month. Sixty percent of all of the prison employees were in the age bracket of 50-70 or over. It reported that only transient drifters or old people could survive on the low prison salaries.

Types of inmates and their crimes have cycled over the years. In 1924 Oklahoma had 52 bank robberies with a loss of $232,000, and hundreds of cars were stolen. The level of fear rose and so did the inmate population. Escapes were common during the early part of the century, but decreased drastically in later years. Prior to 1935 escapes averaged over 100 annually. From 1935 to 1939, the penitentiary recorded 269 escapes. Most escapes were simply "walk-aways" (those who left their outside jobs to visit families or to get drunk at a local bar).

The year 2001 was a record high year for executions conducted in Oklahoma. There were a total of eighteen executions; three were females. Executions in Oklahoma have been performed with lethal injection, however, recently one of the drugs of the three needed for lethal injections has been in short supply. Therefore, it is lawful in Oklahoma to use the electric chair or firing squads for executions.

One particular law passed in 1935 was questionable and unconscionable. It said that "Any person adjudged to be a habitual criminal, shall the adjudication thereof becoming final, be rendered sexually sterile." This statute remained on the books for 14 years. It was not known if this law was ever used, or if any inmate was ever sterilized. This act was eventually ruled unconstitutional by the U.S. Supreme Court in 1949.

In 1939 the State Planning Board recommended that the reformatory at Granite be changed to a maximum institution for 470 of the worst criminals, and that its name be changed to the Western Oklahoma State Penitentiary.

In 1939, political influence, graft, and favors determined whether an inmate remained in the penitentiary or worked in a more pleasing environment.

In 1946 guards were ordered to wear uniforms, and inmates were banned from working in the offices as clerks. These new rules were only partially implemented and were soon forgotten.

Testimony presented to a 1955 House Committee Investigation alleged that availability of drugs and various rackets ran freely at OSP. Gambling, loan sharking, and coffee and ice concessions were controlled by inmate monopolies, and it was not difficult for a shrewd and powerful inmate to generate a savings account in the local bank reaching five figures before he had served his time.

Three individuals in the penal system throughout the years were noteworthy. One served as a warden at a penal institution in Oklahoma, and the other two were notorious inmates in Oklahoma.

Jess Dunn became the warden of the Oklahoma State Penitentiary because of a prison escape. Another escape occurred on Sunday, August 10, 1941. Warden Jess Dunn, three men, and a boy were in the prison yard planning the installation of a communications device to help prevent prison breaks. Four inmates, led by Claude Beavers, armed with a razor, confronted the warden's group near the prison hospital. Beavers said that he was going to cut Warden Dunn's throat; the other inmates forced the other civilians back into the building. With Warden Dunn and one of the men as hostages, Deputy Warden Ben Crider pled with the inmates to release the two men. Crider told them, "Boys, you can't get away with it. If you get through that gate, you'll be killed." In order to meet the inmates' demands, Warden Dunn ordered the guards to lower their weapons on ropes. The guards then lowered two .38 caliber pistols and two .30-.30 rifles, which were later used in the gun battle. The inmates took a car that belonged to a guard, forced the hostage and Dunn into it, but were forced to stop at a washed-out bridge. They then headed south in an attempt to find a way around the bridge. Deputy Sheriff W.E. Alexander, a former guard, had heard the prison-break alarm and recruited Tab Ford, who was a jailer, and Bob Pollock, a city employee. They rushed to the prison to stop the escape. Alexander saw the inmates' car, blocked its path, and jumped out. "Let them pass, Bill," Warden Dunn told him.

Alexander replied, "You can pass Warden, but these convicts have got to get out of that car." Suddenly, the inmates opened fire and a gun battle ensued. Ford was killed by the inmates before he could shoot. Pollock had grabbed a shotgun before leaving town but failed to get shells, leaving Alexander the only armed gunman. Alexander said later he had recalled Warden Dunn instructing guards, "If there should be an escape and I am taken hostage with a knife in my back, if I tell you not to shoot, go ahead and shoot!" Alexander followed that instruction. He killed three of the inmates a short distance from the prison. Warden Dunn was also killed in the shoot-out. The other victims were inmates Claude Beavers of Seminole, Roy McGee of Kay County, and Bill Anderson of Ada, all serving terms for robbery. Inmate Hiram Prather died in the electric chair two years later. The Governor of Oklahoma praised Alexander saying his courageous action probably saved lives. Jess Dunn was remembered as hard as granite when the need arose, but as kindly a man as could be found. Dunn's death saddened even inmates. A statement which was issued by some inmates called Dunn, "The best friend we prisoners ever had. He was the one who lifted us up and held before our eyes hope of self-redemption and placed within our reach the means of its attainment." Jess Dunn Correctional Center, the state's largest minimum-security prison, was named in his honor.

An inmate famous in Oklahoma history was Wiley Post. Wiley was born near Grand Saline, Texas, on November 22, 1899, in a farming family. He was one of five brothers and one sister, had six grades of schooling, professed no religion and did not drink, smoke, or chew tobacco. At age 16 he went to auto mechanic's school in Kansas City paid for by the sale of three bales of cotton. While there, he joined a flying circus and learned to pilot. He wanted to own his own personal airplane. He then came to Oklahoma to work in the oil fields to raise money to buy the plane. In early 1921, he was involved in a robbery and was sentenced to ten years in prison. He was incarcerated at Oklahoma State Reformatory on April 28, 1921. Because of good conduct, he was paroled on June 5, 1922, after which he suffered an accident that caused him the loss of his left eye. He married a girl named Mae Laine. Soon after his marriage, he was hired as a personal pilot to F.C. Hall, a wealthy Chickasha oil man, who purchased a Lockheed Vega 5-C for Wiley. He named the plane "Winnie Mae" after the oil man's daughter. Wiley made the first non-stop flight between the U.S. and Germany. In July of 1933, he completed the first solo flight around the world. During this flight, he set records for the fastest time around the world, the fastest time between New York City and Berlin, and the fastest time across the Atlantic. His first solo flight was across the Bering Sea. He then turned his attention to experimenting with high altitude flying, and he developed the pressurized suit. Wiley and Oklahoma humorist Will Rogers formed a relationship because of mutual interests. They had flown together many times. On their last flight to Russia, via Alaska, their plane crashed near Point Barrow, about 500 miles north of Fairbanks. They were both killed.

An infamous criminal in Oklahoma was the Choctaw Kid, Clarence Carnes, a Choctaw Indian. He served time at OSR for the murder of an Oklahoma service station attendant during a robbery. He and two other men escaped from the reformatory and stole a truck with an elderly couple in it. He was convicted on Federal kidnapping charges and was sentenced to 99 years at the U.S. Penitentiary in Leavenworth, Kansas. He proved to be a disciplinary problem and on July 6, 1945, he was sent to Alcatraz, an island in San Francisco Bay that housed the federal prison. Carnes was 18 at that time and the youngest inmate ever prisoned there. Early the next year, Carnes was drawn into a daring prison escape that quickly went awry. Two guards were wounded. The six inmates who participated seized one cell house. U.S. Marines, on their way home from Okinawa, and prison guards from Leavenworth were sent to help retake the prison. When it was finally over, three of the escapees were dead and two others, Miran Edgar

Thompson and Sam Shockly, were later executed. Carnes was spared the death penalty because he had refused to murder several guards he had been assigned to kill. The bloody escape attempt was the subject of two movies. He died at the Medical Center for Federal Prisoners at Springfield, Montana, on October 3, 1988, at the age of 61. He was buried in a pauper's grave because no one claimed his body. Thus, ended 'Choctaw Kid' OSR #14714.

Warden Jess Dunn started the OSP rodeo in 1940.
He was later killed in a shoot-out in 1941.

Aviator Wiley Post was probably the most famous inmate from OSR. I have personally seen his original record card.

Inmates picking cotton at OSR during World War II

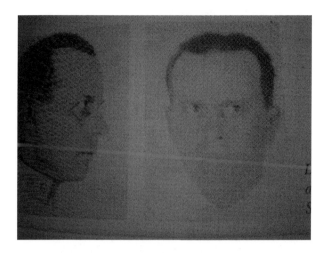

Record card of Doc Barker, a medical doctor,
convicted for murder and sent to OSR

THE DEAD SEA

    Rivers flow and become trapped in the Dead Sea in Israel. This landlocked lake takes but never gives. Because of this, its waters cannot sustain any form of life. However, in the same area, lakes accept and release the river waters. These lakes are teeming with life because they give, as well as receive. Human life is like the Dead Sea and its surrounding bodies of water. Takers do know how to give without an ulterior motive. These people who take but cannot or will not give are often found in prisons.

The Dead Sea in Israel

MICHAEL A. NORCROSS

CONCLUSION

I hope I have fulfilled my purpose in portraying the various duties of a Recreational Supervisor in a penal institution. I enjoyed my years in that capacity, even though it was very stressful to staff and inmates as well. Recreation is enjoyable to inmates and helps to reduce their stress. My co-workers and I got along well with the inmates because they were engaged in something enjoyable. Recreation is so important in a prison setting to eliminate meaningless time. Everyone knows that "Idleness is the Devil's workshop." The more time inmates were involved in recreation the less trouble we had and the fewer "write ups" were issued.

I think educating and understanding people before they commit crimes are the keys to reducing the prison population. However, recreation teaches inmates to cope better if sent to prison. I also feel the inmate will be more productive when discharged. I hope that I have made a difference in people's lives who have been incarcerated. There is cursing in this book, although not by me. Anyone would expect inmates to curse. I am a religious person and have quoted two Bible scriptures in this book. I think more spiritual training, spiritual meditation, and lessons from the Bible would alleviate crime. After all, the word recreation means Re-Creation.

Back Cover: Michael rings the bell.

Made in the USA
Charleston, SC
03 February 2017